Building Christian Confidence

EVA GIBSON AND STEVE PRICE

BETHANY HOUSE PUBLISHERS

MINNEAPOLIS, MINNESOTA 55438

A Division of Bethany Fellowship, Inc.

Dedicated to
Joann Price,
who encouraged us from the beginning.

A special thank you to
Beth Niquette
for teaching section one to her teen Sunday school class at
the Olalla Bible Church in Washington.

A special acknowledgment to Zane Hodges for material from *The Hungry Inherit*
by Multnomah Press © 1980 used in Lessons 29, 31, 32, and 34.

Except where noted, all scripture quotations in this publications are from the *Holy Bible, New International Version.* Copyright © 1973, 1978, International Bible Society. Used by permission of Zondervan Bible Publishers.

ISBN 0–87123–934–5

Published by Bethany House Publishers
A Division of Bethany Fellowship, Inc.
6820 Auto Club Road, Minneapolis, Minnesota 55438

Printed in the United States of America

CONTENTS

INTRODUCTION

Some of our hymns refer to us as a *wretch* or *worm*. The world says we are exalted and great beings, the highest order in an evolutionary scale. They say that we have the power to do all things. We just have to reach down inside ourselves—find the good within, the god inside—and develop our "God-consciousness."

The Bible tells us that we are sinners, depraved and separated from God, in ourselves unable to know Him and live a life pleasing to Him. It also tells us we are of infinite worth in the eyes of God because He sent His Son to die for us.

What is the balance between our view and God's view of our sinfulness and of our view and God's view of our worth?

The goal of this book is to teach an accurate picture of our God and ourselves based on His Word.

SECTION I

SEEING MY PARTNERSHIP: THE NAMES AND CHARACTER OF GOD HELP ME SEE MY RESOURCES

"If God is for us, who can be against us?" (Rom. 8:31).

Section Objective: To gain an accurate perspective of who we are by first understanding who God is.

LESSON 1

KNOWING GOD

A. WHAT DOES IT MEAN TO KNOW GOD?

1. When you say you know someone, what do you mean? _____
   _____

2. What does it take to really know a person?_____
   _____

3. What do you think J. I. Packer means when he says, "Knowing God . . . is a more complex business than knowing a fellowman"? (See Isa. 55:8)_____
   _____

4. The Bible helps us understand what knowing God means. We can know God as a son knows his father, a wife her husband, a subject his king, a sheep his shepherd. Yet even with these analogies, God is so great He can't reveal himself to us all at once.
   a. What does Jesus say about knowing God? (John 14:6–9)_____
      _____

   b. Look at John 10:27. What does Christ say are the results of knowing Him?_____

   c. Jesus uses another analogy to explain the gift He wants to give each of us. What is it? (John 4:10, 13, 14)
      _____

B. THINKING IT THROUGH (ISAIAH 55)

1. What does it mean to thirst for God? (vv. 1, 2)_____
   _____

2. Our dilemma: we don't know that we thirst. Yet God's Word reveals that we're created to thirst for God, that there is within each of us a God-implanted need to have fellowship with Him.

   Complete the following diagram of the soul. Label the broken circle "body"; the heart-shaped section, the "soul"; the three-part sections "mind," "intellect" and "will." Put "God" in the upper right-hand corner and draw an arrow between His name and the circled center. Label the center, "Spirit."

3. Closely examine
    a. God's invitation. (Isa. 55:1–5; John 6:35, 45–51)
        What is the condition of those being invited?_____
        Who's doing the inviting?_____
    b. List the benefits for those who respond to the invitation. (Isa. 44:2–4; Ezek. 36:25–27)_____
    _____

4. Write out Ps. 42:1–2_____
    _____

    _____

5. Do we really long for God like the deer longs for the water? If we're honest, we have to recognize that even after we've become God's child, we don't always thirst for Him. Our flesh puts shadows in our lives, holds us away from being satisfied with Him.
    Return to #2. Add several dark shadows to the diagram to illustrate this truth.

6. How is the thirst for God different from the thirst for the things of this world?_____
    _____

    Contrast the world's way of satisfying with the water offered in Isa. 55:1, 2_____
    _____

7. This outline of Isaiah 55 is given to help you think through the seven steps of how to satisfy your thirst for God. Find the scripture verse or verses that go with each point.

Title: Drinking Deep from the Right Well

1) Realizing my need   _____
2) Recognizing the truth   _____
3) Responding in time   _____
4) Repenting of sin   _____
5) Resting in God   _____
6) Receiving new life   _____
7) Rejoicing in assurance   _____

C. CONTEMPORARY APPLICATION

Do you see kids at school looking for satisfaction in worldly pursuits? What are these pursuits? What do you think the end results will be? What would be the end results if those same lives were spent thirsting after God, seeking satisfaction from Him?

D. VERSES TO THINK ON THIS WEEK

Jer. 9:23–24; Matt. 5:6; Eph. 1:17–20; Rev. 21:6; 22:17

E. THOUGHT TO CARRY HOME

Our quest for God will intensify as it moves along. We've learned that the same God who creates the thirst quenches it by the work of the Spirit. We furnish the parched throat. He supplies the living water.

F. CREATIVE EXPRESSION

Express your thirst for God in a personal psalm to God. If you're in a dry spot, pour out that dryness instead. Be honest with God. Tell it like it is. (Use Psalm 42 or 43 as a pattern.)
OR
Look up the following verses and list the benefits that come to those who seek God: Ps. 8:1, 9; 9:1–2; 9:9–10; 20:5, 7; 22:22; 33:21; 34:3; 34:10; 37:4; 42:1. Spend time meditating on each verse.

_____

_____

_____

_____

G. SELF-EVALUATION

1. Do I recognize that it is the God who knows and loves me who is seeking me?
2. How does it make me feel to realize that the God who made me wants me to know Him in a personal way?
3. Do I recognize God as my Father? my king? my shepherd?
4. Have I asked God to create a thirst in me?
5. Can I honestly say, "Jesus is my best friend"? Do I want to say it?
6. Have I taken the seven necessary steps to satisfy my thirst?

LESSON 2

MY *ELOHIM*, THE MIGHTY CREATOR

A. *ELOHIM*, GOD OF CREATION.

1. The word *Elohim* means mighty, strong, prominent. In Num. 23:22 (KJV) *God* is spoken of as having the strength of an _____ . Ps. 89:13 refers to _____
2. *Elohim* also means to declare or swear. It implies a covenant relationship. A covenant is a clear statement of what God will do solely based on His sovereign action.
   It also signifies God's commitment to His people. This commitment is best illustrated in the_____ relationship (Isa. 54:5; Jer. 31:31–33). God says He'll be a _____ to His people.

B. THINKING IT THROUGH (GEN. 1:1–2)

1. How do you picture verses 1 and 2? Write a picture sentence describing it._____
   _____
   _____
2. Who, according to John 1:2, 10; Col. 2:9; and Heb. 1:10, participated in creation?_____
3. Who moved across the face of the waters?_____
4. Gen. 3:3–31 gives us a picture of God creating. We see *Elohim* working and being.

   List His three creative acts:
   1._____
   2._____
   3._____

   List the three persons of the Godhead:
   1._____
   2._____
   3._____

5. These creative acts show His power, majesty and greatness. Nathan Stone, a professor at Moody Bible Institute, says, "It is most appropriate that by this name [*Elohim*] God should reveal Himself—bringing *cosmos* out of *chaos, light* out of *darkness, habitation* out of *desolation*, and life in His image."
   With the help of a dictionary, write down key thoughts for the words underlined in the quote. Contrast them.
   _____
   _____
   _____

6. God's first creative act on earth was to create _____ (Gen. 1:3).
   a. How can darkness be a picture of a life without God?_____
      _____
   b. Can it be that one reason we fear darkness is that it's a picture of sin and self? Respond to this statement: "God is light; self is darkness." Agree? Disagree?
      _____
      _____

c. What characteristics of light can you relate to God?_____

_____

_____

7. The personal nature of God is expressed in the opening chapters of Genesis. Discover from the verses below the truths that show God as a living person, thinking, feeling, interested in His creatures.
   a. Gen. 3:8_____
   b. Gen. 3:8_____
   c. Gen. 3:9_____
   d. Gen. 3:11, 13_____
   e. Gen. 6:6_____

8. Knowing God begins with a new relationship. We can choose light over darkness, for God has the power to pick us up out of the kingdom of darkness and place us in a new kingdom, the kingdom of light (Eph. 1:17–23).
   a. To have light is to see, recognize, know. How can understanding that truth help you comprehend who God is?_____

   _____

   _____

   _____

   b. How can I let His light change me?_____

   _____

C. CONTEMPORARY APPLICATION

How would you respond if someone in your science class said to you, "I'll believe in God when I see Him"? Try to answer that statement by thinking through the following questions: How would you describe spiritual light and darkness? Could you liken it to scientific truth? What changes has God's light already made in your life? in the lives of some of the Christian kids in your class?

D. VERSES TO THINK ON THIS WEEK

John 17:3; Eph. 1:17–18; Phil. 3:10; 1 Pet. 2:9–10; 1 Chron. 28:9

E. THOUGHT TO CARRY HOME

Recognizing God's creative power helps me realize His light. To have light means to see—recognize. To know God in the fullest sense of the word.

F. CREATIVE EXPRESSION

Do an acrostic on the word light. Choose words that describe characteristics of Elohim that will help you remember who He is and what He is like.

_____ L _____

_____ I _____

_____ G _____

_____ H _____

_____ T _____

G. SELF-EVALUATION

1. How can knowing God as the God of light help me better understand Him myself?
2. In what ways would I like to experience His light? His creative power within me?
3. How can an understanding of God's creative power living in me change me?
4. Has His Spirit shown me an area of darkness (self-centeredness, sin) today?
5. If He has, how can I let Him penetrate that darkness?
6. How can I become a light-bringer that exhibits ever-increasing clarity?

LESSON 3

MY *JEHOVAH*, THE REDEEMER

A. *JEHOVAH*, THE SELF-EXISTENT I AM

Jehovah occurs 6,823 times in the Old Testament. In most translations it has been translated LORD (all capitals) to distinguish it from *Adonai*, also translated Lord.

The name *Jehovah* is derived from the Hebrew noun *havah*, which means "to be," or "being." This is almost exactly like the Hebrew verb *chavah*, "to live" or "life."

Truth simplified: *Jehovah* is the cause of His own being. He is independent and complete in himself, needing no one. He is the kernel, or center, of who God is. All other names radiate out from it.

B. THINKING IT THROUGH

Climbing the acrostic ladder. Begin at the bottom and complete this acrostic as you answer the questions below:

```
              J _____
        _____ E _____
              H _____
     _____ O _____
        _____ V _____
     _____ A _____
              H _____  _____
```

1. "H"
   a. Discover Moses' plight in Ex. 2:14–15. What is he feeling? Write down key words that focus in on his emotions. _____

   _____

   b. Discover the Israelites' condition. Write down key words describing them. (Ex. 1:10–14, 22; 2:23–25)

   _____

   _____

   c. Acrostic clue. Description of a _____ _____ (Ps. 77:1–2)

2. "A"
   a. How does God reveal himself to Moses? (Ex. 3) _____

   _____

   b. What is Moses' response? _____

   _____

   c. What is God's response to Moses? _____

   _____

   _____

   d. Acrostic clue: Anytime God wished to make a special revelation of himself, He used the name *Jehovah*. "This name is not simply a label for identification, but much more profoundly a revelation of the divine nature" (T. A. Bryant).

3. "V"
   a. What do we see God doing in Gen. 3:8–9? _____

   b. It's your turn to seek Him. Read Judg. 10:16; Isa. 63:9; Jer. 31:3; Hos. 11:1–4; Eph. 3:17–18. Using these verses as references, write a description of *Jehovah's* love. Personalize it, using your own words. _____

   _____

   _____

   _____

   c. Acrostic clue: 1 John 4:8

4. "O"

    a. Write down the attributes of God that reveal His love in Ex. 34:5–7 _____

    _____

    _____

    _____

    b. These attributes point us to _____ , the ultimate sacrifice. (Heb. 1:1–3)

    c. Acrostic clue: In Heb. 2:10, Jesus is called the author of our _____ .

5. "H"

    a. We can't lose sight of *Jehovah's* holiness as we view His love. To Israel, righteousness and holiness were the two great attributes associated with the name *Jehovah*.

      1) In Gen. 3:23–24, we see God_____

      2) In Gen. 19:24, we see Him raining burning sulphur upon _____ and _____

    b. *Jehovah's* holiness cannot look at _____ (Hab. 1:13)

    c. The result of sin is _____ (Rom. 6:23)

    d. What is the paradox that we see in Isa. 45:21?_____

    _____

    e. Acrostic clue: 1 Chron. 16:29

6. "E"

    a. Look up the word *redeem* in the dictionary. Write down the definition or definitions you feel most closely explain the biblical meaning._____

    _____

    _____

    b. Because Jehovah is both a just God and Savior, He sent Jesus to_____

    _____ . (1 Pet. 1:18–20; Rev. 5:9)

7. "J"

    a. Put into your own words the I AM truth of Exodus 3._____

    _____

    _____

    b. Look up the I AMs in the Gospel of John. Jesus said, "I am the _____ ____ _____ (6:35), _____ ____ ____ _____ (8:12), _____ (10:9), _____ _____ (10:11), _____ _____ _____ _____ (11:25), _____ , _____ _____ , _____ _____ (14:6), _____ _____ (15:1)

    c. Note the reaction of the Pharisees when Jesus said, "Before Abraham was, I am (John 8:58, KJV). Do you think they understood what Jesus was saying? Why or why not?_____

    _____

    d. Additional acrostic clue: Dr. Herbert Lockyer says that the letters *JE* represent the word Jehovah, indicating that Jesus is God. The syllable SUS is a derivative of names meaning "to help." *Jesus*, therefore, means "the help of God," or "the salvation of God."

C. CONTEMPORARY APPLICATION

Think about the meaning of *Jehovah—Jesus*, my powerful redeemer and helper. Are you facing situations at school where you need to be reminded of this name? At home? Describe one and tell how knowing Jesus as Jehovah could make this aspect of who He is real to you, even change your attitude regarding it. How might it even change the situation?

D. VERSES TO THINK ON THIS WEEK

Ex. 3:14; Isa. 45:22–24; John 1:14; 8:12; Rev. 2:28

E. THOUGHT TO CARRY HOME

Jehovah's very name reveals that the cross was in the mind of God before the world began. This truth walks with us through the pages of His Word, leaving a crimson path for us to follow.

F. CREATIVE EXPRESSION

Ask your God the question, "Who are you, Lord?" Answer it by finishing the sentence I AM . . . with truth you've discovered today. Personalize it to your own needs.

I Am . . . _____

_____

_____

G. SELF-EVALUATION

1. How much does God want me?
2. How much do I need Him?
3. Do I recognize the price God paid for my redemption? Do I see how valuable I am? how precious I am in His sight?
4. Am I the only person worthy of this redemption?
5. If all people are of equal value, how should I respond to others?
6. How can I show my parents that I value them this week? other family members? my friends?

LESSON 4

MY *EL SHADDAI*, SUFFICIENT FOR ALL MY NEEDS

A. *EL SHADDAI*, MIGHTY GOD

The name *El* for God is especially connected with power and might. Many scholars believe *Shaddai* is derived from the word *breast*. Then *Shaddai* (one who nourishes, supplies, and satisfies) connected with *El* describes God as the one mighty to nourish, satisfy, and supply.

B. THINKING IT THROUGH

1. The first occurrence of the name *El Shaddai* is in Gen. 17:1. How old is Abraham when he is given the promise that he would have a son?_____

2. How does Heb. 11:12 describe Abraham at this point in his life?_____

_____

3. What are the specifics in God's promises to Abraham? (Gen. 17:2–8)
   a. _____
   b. _____
   c. _____
   d. _____
   e. _____
   f. _____

4. Out of the 48 times it appears in the Old Testament, the name *El Shaddai* occurs 31 times in the Book of Job.
   a. God permitted the testing of Job, not in judgment, but to purify him for greater fruitfulness. Compare Job's beginning with his ending (Also read Job 5:17–18; Eph. 3:19.)

   Beginning (Job 1:1–3)   Ending (Job 42:10–17)

   _____   _____

   b. What was Job's attitude toward suffering? (Job 13:15)_____

   _____

   c. Compare Naomi's beginning with her ending (Also read Heb. 12:1–12.)

   Beginning (Ruth 1:1–5)   Ending (Ruth 4:14–16, 22)

   _____   _____

   d. What was Naomi's attitude toward suffering? (Ruth 1:21)_____

   _____

e. What positives resulted in Job's and Naomi's lives because of God's chastening?

Job's	Naomi's
1) _____	1) _____
2) _____	2) _____

5. What positive results can we expect from God's chastening? (Heb. 12:1–15)_____

6. Draw a simple picture of the truth expressed in John 12:24.
7. Finish these sentences:
   a. Seeds must die before a _____ sprouts.
   b. Grapes must be crushed before _____ is produced.
   c. Wheat must be ground before it's made into _____ .
   d. Vines must be pruned before they produce _____ .
   e. I must die to my selfish desires before_____

8. Note the progression in fruit-bearing in John 15:1–5: _____ , _____ , _____
9. What is my responsibility in fruit-bearing? (Gal. 6:9–10)_____

10. Personalize the truth of John 15:5b and Phil. 4:13. Substitute the word *Jesus* for Him, your own name for you.

11. Jesus also said He was the bread of life (John 6:35). How can you tie this truth in with the Old Testament name *El Shaddai?*_____

C. CONTEMPORARY APPLICATION

1. Many things have been promoted by our society as "needs," yet our actual needs are very basic. Discern between the "wants" and "needs" in your own life by asking yourself, "What are the actual essentials for life?" "What are merely fringe benefits?"
2. List three basic needs: _____ , _____ , _____
3. God not only meets our physical needs, He's willing to meet our spiritual needs, too. Since He's everything we need for an abundant life, then He's everything our friends need, too. Personalize:
   a. I can be an encouragement to _____ by sharing what Jesus means to me by_____
   b. Another person who comes into my mind when I think of being an encourager is _____ (Heb. 10:24). I can spur on _____ this week by_____

D. VERSES TO THINK ON THIS WEEK
John 15:5 *with* Phil. 4:13; John 6:35; Eph. 1:18–20; Heb. 13:20–21

E. THOUGHT TO CARRY HOME
Jesus is my *El Shaddai*, sufficient for my every need.

F. CREATIVE EXPRESSION
Finish this sentence: Because Jesus is my *El Shaddai* and the bread of life, I can . . . _____

G. SELF-EVALUATION
1. What do I really need?
2. Have I experienced the heart hunger to bear fruit?

3. What fruit listed in Gal. 5:22–23 do I need most in my life right now? Have I asked God to cultivate this in me?

4. If I have, have I realized obedience isn't always easy? Have I seen that chastening is a prerequisite for fruitfulness?

5. How does Jesus' teaching in John 12:24 relate to my life right now? to the goals in my life?

LESSON 5

MY *ABBA*, A FATHER TO THE FATHERLESS

A. DEFINE A FATHER.

_____
_____
_____
_____

B. THINKING IT THROUGH

You may not know your father or have what you consider to be a good father figure. The following illustrates the sufficiency of God to be your perfect Father.

1. The promise of God.

   What do these verses say about God's promise to care for us (to be our Father)?

   a. Ps. 68:5–6_____

   b. Isa. 64:8_____

   c. Matt. 6:9_____

   Summary: None of us has a perfect father, and some may not even know their father, but we see that God wants to be a Father to all. Examine the following four areas that exemplify God as our Father.

2. The person of God.

   a. What do these verses say about God as our provider?

   Deut. 10:17–18_____

   Ps. 34:7–10_____

   Ps. 146:9_____

   Matt. 6:25–34_____

   b. What do these verses say about God as our teacher?

   Ps. 25:4–5_____

   Ps. 32:8_____

   Isa. 2:3_____

John 14:26_____

_____

   c. What do these verses say about God as our protector?
     Ex. 22:22–24_____

_____

     2 Chron. 16:9_____

_____

     Ps. 10:17–18_____

_____

     Rom. 8:31, 37–39_____

_____

   d. What do these verses say about God as our nurturer?
     Jer. 31:3_____

_____

     John 3:16_____

_____

     Rom. 5:8_____

_____

     1 John 4:10–11, 19_____

_____

3. Describe the relationship between the Father and His children as explained in 1 John 3:1–3._____

_____

_____

C. CONTEMPORARY APPLICATION

Think of the men you know. Do any of them have one or more of the above characteristics? Pick out an action or an incident you've observed that models each one (provider, protector, teacher and nurturer) and write about it._____

_____

_____

_____

_____

_____

_____

D. VERSES TO THINK ON THIS WEEK

Ps. 68:5; 32:8; 2 Chron. 16:9; Jer. 31:3

E. THOUGHT TO CARRY HOME

Regardless of our family situation, God is our Father, and He is a perfect Father. When we feel fatherless or "let down," we can claim the provision, teaching, protection, and love offered by God, our heavenly Father.

F. CREATIVE EXPRESSION

Write a prayer to God expressing the areas in which you feel you need to see Him as your Father. Thank Him that He is always there as your Father regardless of any circumstances.
    OR

If you're not sure you're a child of God, write a prayer paraphrasing these verses (John 1:12; 3:16; Rom. 3:23; 5:8) in your own words, asking Him to make you part of His family.

_____

_____

_____

_____

G. SELF-EVALUATION

1. How do I know that God is a perfect Father?
2. Am I willing to commit myself totally into God's hands, knowing He will care for me?
3. Do I trust God enough to be my Father?
4. How do I see the Fatherhood of God expressed in other scripture passages?
5. How have I seen His Fatherhood expressed in the daily circumstances of my life? Can I think of a specific example?
6. Have I prayed honestly, acknowledging God as my Father?

LESSON 6

MY *ADONAI*, THE LORD OF MY LIFE

A. DEFINE *ADONAI*

Adonai, like *Elohim*, is almost always in the plural. It confirms the trinity and is almost always possessive, recognizing ownership.

1. God first reveals himself to Abram as *Adonai* (Gen. 15:1–6). The first two words in the chapter are: _____ _____ .

2. After what? Go back to chapter 14. Discover Abram's position._____
   _____
   _____

3. Because Abram was in authority over others, he knew what ownership and lordship meant. When he addresses God as Sovereign LORD (the original Hebrew renders it *Adonai Jehovah*), he is acknowledging_____
   _____

B. THINKING IT THROUGH

Learning from the lives of those who recognized God as their Lord (*Adonai*), Master, and Owner.

1. Moses (Ex. 4:1–17)
   a. What does Moses fear? (v. 1)_____
   b. Moses addresses *Jehovah* as Lord (*Adonai*)—his Master and Owner—but he still rejects his Master's words. What are his objections? (v. 10)_____
   _____
   c. What does God promise to do for his reluctant servant? (v. 12)_____
   _____
   d. Why does God become angry when Moses still persists in holding back? (vv. 14–17)_____
   _____

2. Joshua (Josh. 7:6–15)
   a. What happens after Joshua acknowledges God as his Master (*Adonai*) and pours out his problem to him?
   _____
   b. Either draw a cartoon or outline the steps of action God gave Joshua. Show Joshua's response.

3. David (2 Sam. 7:18–29; Ps. 139:1–4, 23)
   a. What words in David's prayer reflect his attitude toward God?_____
   _____
   _____
   b. What does David call himself?_____
   c. His God?_____
   d. Turn to Ps. 139:1–4, 23. What is repeated several times? _____ What does this tell you about your God?_____
   _____

4. The prophets (Isa. 6:1–8; Jer. 1:4–10; Dan. 9:19)
   a. Write a description of Isaiah's vision (Isa. 6:1–8)_____
   _____
   _____
   _____
   b. Write his response to the Lord's glory (v. 5)_____
   _____
   _____
   c. How does he respond to God's call to service? (v. 8)_____
   _____
   d. What is Jeremiah's objection to God's appointment? (Jer. 1:6)_____
   _____
   e. What are God's instructions? (v. 7)_____
   _____
   f. His promises? (v. 8)_____
   g. What is the significance of God touching both prophets' mouths?_____
   _____
   h. Daniel knows his people have sinned against their Master, *Adonai*. In Daniel 9 the prophet addresses his prayer to *Adonai*, pleading for forgiveness, acceptance, and restoration. Rewrite verse 19 by replacing the word Lord with *Adonai*._____
   _____
   _____

5. Jesus (John 12:26; 13:1–17)
   a. Discover in which verses Jesus reveals himself to His disciples as both Lord and Servant. Write them here.
   _____
   _____
   b. What other nouns does Jesus use here to help the disciples understand who He is? (John 13:12–16)
   _____
   c. What does Jesus promise to those who follow His example? (John 13:17)_____
   _____
   d. What characteristics of servanthood does Jesus model for us? (Matt. 20:26–28; Luke 22:27; John 8:29; Rom. 15:3; Phil. 2:7–8; Heb. 10:7)_____
   _____
   _____
   _____

C. CONTEMPORARY APPLICATION

Have I turned myself over to God as a servant, willing to serve out of love with no concern for reward? If I declare Jesus to be my Lord, *Adonai*, why can't I say, "No, Lord"? Why is that a contradictory statement? What is a better response?

D. VERSES TO THINK ON THIS WEEK

Ps. 123:2; Isa. 6:7–8; John 12:26; Rev. 22:12

E. THOUGHT TO CARRY HOME

"The throne of God and of the Lamb will be in the city, and his servants will serve him. They will see his face, and his name will be on their foreheads. There will be no more night. They will not need the light of a lamp or the light of the sun, for the Lord God will give them light. And they will reign for ever and ever" (Rev. 22: 3b–5).

F. CREATIVE EXPRESSION

As a practical expression of servanthood, ask God to bring into your mind someone He wants you to be a servant to this week. Ask Him to give you a creative way to serve that person. Write that idea in your workbook. Then write a prayer asking God to help you follow through._____

_____

_____

_____

G. SELF-EVALUATION

1. How am I like Moses? Where do I see myself as inadequate? Is God sufficient for these areas?
2. In what areas do I need to ask God for cleansing and forgiveness?
3. Have I poured out my feelings before Him and allowed Him to teach me?
4. How thoroughly does God know me? Will He give me the power to do what He asks of me?
5. Is there any other part of creation that can worship and serve God? Why does God have the right of ownership on my life?
6. Do I realize His majesty and might on the one hand, His servant heart on the other? What difference will this understanding make in my life?

LESSON 7

MY *JEHOVAH-ROHI*, THE GREAT SHEPHERD

A. *JEHOVAH-ROHI*, THE GREAT SHEPHERD

Jehovah-Rohi, appears in Psalm 23. The primary meaning of this name is to feed or lead to pasture, as a shepherd does his sheep.

Rohi has been translated *companion* or *friend* and expresses the intimacy of sharing life, food, etc. It is the word for friend in Ex. 33:11, where it says, "The Lord would speak to Moses face to face, as a man speaks with his friend."

1. Nathan describes the closeness of a man and his sheep in 2 Sam. 12:3. What family relationship does he liken it to?_____

2. *Jehovah-Rohi* reveals two aspects of God's personality. On one hand is His power, majesty, and greatness; on the other, His tender, compassionate shepherd heart. The creative power of Jehovah is clearly portrayed in Isaiah 40. Near the middle of the chapter is a single verse that reveals His shepherd's heart. Write the verse.

_____

_____

_____

B. THINKING IT THROUGH

1. *Jehovah-Rohi* first appears in Psalm 23, written by David. Look up the following verses and write down what David knew about being a shepherd.

   1 Sam. 16:11, 19_____

   1 Sam. 17:15, 34–36_____

   2 Sam. 7:8_____

2. Which of God's character qualities are revealed in Psalm 23?_____
_____
_____

3. Discover from the Word more of what a shepherd is like.
   Gen. 48:15_____
   Gen. 49:24_____
   1 Kings 22:17_____
   Ps. 100:3_____
   Ps. 121:5, 6_____
   Ezek. 34:16_____
   Matt. 9:36_____
   Luke 15:4–7_____

4. How can you apply these truths to Jesus, the Great Shepherd?_____
_____
_____

5. A closer look at the Good Shepherd in John 10:
   a. What additional truth does John 10 show you about the shepherd work of Jesus Christ?_____
   _____
   _____

   b. What words would you use to describe Jesus as the Shepherd?_____
   _____
   _____

   c. One way to help you gain an understanding of the Shepherd's responsibility for you and your responsibility to Him is to finish these sentences. The first one is done for you.
   His part is . . .
      1) to know His sheep
      2) _____
      3) _____
   My part is . . .
      1) _____
      2) _____
      3) _____

6. Note the progression in these verses: Jesus is the _____ Shepherd (John 10:14), the _____ Shepherd (Heb. 13:20), the _____ Shepherd (1 Pet. 5:4).
   Look up the dictionary definition of *chief*. Write down the part you feel describes God._____
   _____
   _____

7. Jesus became that Good, Great, Chief Shepherd by first becoming a lamb. He identified himself so totally with us, His sheep, that He became the Lamb of God who takes away the sin of the world. Write down the following verses:
   Isa. 53:6, 7_____
   _____
   _____

   John 1:29_____
   _____

C. CONTEMPORARY APPLICATION

We live in a society with voices that shout for attention, distracting us and demanding our time. The most significant voice is a quiet one, the voice of the Shepherd. He asks that we put all else aside and listen.

The Shepherd knows His sheep, but the sheep must pause to know the Shepherd, to learn His ways, and to receive the comfort, guidance, and protection they need in a world that sometimes hates them.

D. VERSES TO THINK ON THIS WEEK

Ps. 23:1; Isa. 40:11; Ezek. 34:11; John 10:11; Rev. 7:17

E. THOUGHT TO CARRY HOME

My Shepherd knows me by name. He knows my particular needs, my peculiarities, my weaknesses. Because He does, I can trust Him.

F. CREATIVE EXPRESSION

Compare Psalm 23, with the heavenly scene described in Rev. 7:15–17 where Jesus is revealed as the Lamb on the throne. Pick out similar phrases from both scriptures. Example:

Ps. 23	Rev. 7:15–17
The Lord is my shepherd	The Lamb at the center of the throne is the shepherd

How does this heavenly scene deepen your understanding of *Jehovah-Rohi*, our Shepherd Jesus? How does it make you feel to realize that this Shepherd who gave His life for you is alive, enthroned in glory, and eagerly listening to hear your words?_____

_____

_____

G. SELF-EVALUATION

1. What other voices compete with the voice of my Shepherd?
2. How can I learn to draw close to my Shepherd? to hear His voice more clearly?
3. Am I daily cultivating my relationship with Him?
4. How can I recognize His voice the way He longs for me to do?
5. In what areas can I trust Him more and be more obedient to Him?
6. Have I talked to my Shepherd today?

LESSON 8

THE SUN OF RIGHTEOUSNESS, JESUS CHRIST

A. WHO IS THE SUN OF RIGHTEOUSNESS? (MAL. 4:1–3)

God created the sun and uses the creation to reveal himself. (Rom. 1:20)

1. What characteristics does the sun have that can be applied to Jesus?_____

_____

_____

2. Read John 1:1–9 and note the number of times Jesus is referred to as light. How many did you discover?

_____

3. Contrast Prov. 4:18 *with* 4:19.

"The path of the righteous is like_____."

"The way of the wicked is like_____."

B. THINKING IT THROUGH

Righteousness: right being, right thinking, right doing.

1. How are the righteous acts we try to do on our own described? (Isa. 64:6)_____

_____

2. Where does true righteousness lie? (Isa. 45:24; 1 Cor. 1:30)_____

_____

3. On whom does the Sun of Righteousness shine?_____

   a. What are the results of His shining? 1) _____ 2) _____

   b. How can I let His holy rays penetrate my life in practical ways?

      Ps. 139:23_____

      1 John 1:9_____

      Heb. 4:15–16_____

   c. What are two other results of letting His holiness penetrate our lives? (Mal. 4:2, 3)

      1)_____

      2)_____

4. What part does the vinedresser have in the vine's production?

   a. Read John 15:1–10 and list the vinedresser's responsibilities._____

_____

_____

_____

   b. List His purposes (John 15:8; Phil. 1:11)

      1) _____

      2) _____

5. What does it mean to be fruitful in our Christian lives?

   a. Read John 15:7–10 and list the qualities of a fruitful life.

      1) _____

      2) _____

      3) _____

      4) _____

   b. Read John 14:15–21 and discover the source of our fruitfulness. List the character qualities produced by Him when we live a life of obedience. (Gal. 5:22, 23)_____

_____

_____

6. One of the results of fruitfulness is fragrance. Compare John 15:1–5 with Song of Songs (Song of Solomon) 4:16. Who is producing the fragrance within us?_____

   a. How do we go about applying the fragrance and strength of the Holy Spirit? (Matt. 14:22–23; Mark 1:35)

_____

   b. What is the result of spending time with God? (2 Cor. 3:7–11, 18)_____

   c. What are some of the fragrance robbers that Eccles. 10:1 warns us against? Name some specific "flies" that you see robbing you of spiritual strength and fragrance._____

_____

_____

7. Christ's fragrance is produced in us through the discipline of hard times.

   a. What does the crushed grape produce besides juice?_____

   b. Mal. 3:2 shows us a picture of God as a _____ and a_____.

c. What is the Holy Spirit's purpose in allowing discipline and pain in our lives?_____
_____
_____

d. What does God ultimately desire to accomplish in our lives through suffering?
2 Cor. 4:6–10_____
_____
_____

2 Cor. 2:14–16_____
_____
_____

C. CONTEMPORARY APPLICATION

Some famous personalities have fragrances named after them. Name a few. What are the connotations of some of them? What lies behind the lives of those they represent? Purity? Impurity? Holiness? Unholiness?

Think about your life. If you had a fragrance named after you, what would it be? What would it represent? How would it reflect your relationship with God?

D. VERSES TO THINK ON THIS WEEK

Mal. 4:2; John 1:4; 2 Cor. 2:14; 3:18

E. THOUGHT TO CARRY HOME

As we allow the Sun of Righteousness to shine into our lives, He purifies us with His holiness. This healing sunshine produces purity and a fruitfulness that carries a distinct fragrance. A purified, fruitful person is a light in a dark world.

F. CREATIVE EXPRESSION

Pick out the scent that came to your mind as you thought through the application questions on what kind of fragrance you'd like your life to have if it could be bottled. Write several descriptive sentences of your choice, then explain why you chose that particular scent._____
_____
_____
_____

G. SELF-EVALUATION

1. In what ways would you like to experience more of the Sun of Righteousness in your life?
2. Are you willing to spend time in His presence, allowing His righteousness to penetrate your personality?
3. What fruit of the Spirit do you feel is most lacking in your life?
4. Are you willing to take that need to Him and ask Him to produce that fruit within you?
5. What are the dead flies you listed in 6c? Are you willing to lay them out before the Sun of Righteousness and claim the promise of 1 John 1:9?
7. Are you willing to pray, "Lord Jesus, make my life a fragrance for Your glory"? What might it cost you to pray such a prayer?

SECTION II
SEEING MY PERSON: GAINING AN ACCURATE PERSPECTIVE OF WHO I AM

"Let us make man in our image, in our likeness" (Gen. 1:26).

Section Objective: To gain from God's Word an accurate perspective of who we are.

LESSON 9

UNDERSTANDING THE BEGINNING

A. CONTRAST THE TWO WORLDS

Before the Fall Gen. 1:1–31	After the Fall Gen. 3:14, 17–19; Rom. 8:22–23
_____	_____
_____	_____
_____	_____

B. THINKING IT THROUGH

1. Before the fall
   a. What was God's view of Adam and Eve? (Gen. 1:8–25, 31; 3:8)_____
   _____

   b. What was Adam and Eve's view of God? (Gen. 2:16, 18–22; 3:8)_____
   _____
   _____

   c. What was Adam and Eve's view of one another? (Gen. 2:23–25)_____
   _____
   _____

2. After the fall
   a. What was God's view of Adam and Eve? (Gen. 3:8–13, 15, 21)_____
   _____

   b. What was Adam and Eve's view of God? (Gen. 3:10–24)_____
   _____
   _____

   c. What was their view of each other? (Gen. 3:16–19; 4:1–8)_____
   _____
   _____

C. CONTEMPORARY APPLICATION

Sin separated Adam and Eve from God and from each other. Sin still separates. It separates families, countries, and nations.

1. What examples of the separation caused by sin are in the news today?_____
2. In families you know?_____
3. What do the separations Adam and Eve experienced tell me about myself?_____
4. What happens when I let sin control me?_____
5. What effect does it have on me? my family? my friends? my relationship with God?_____
_____
6. What hope were Adam and Eve given? (Gen. 3:15)_____
_____
7. What does this hope mean to me?_____
_____
_____

D. VERSES TO THINK ON THIS WEEK

Gen. 1:26; Ps. 100:3; 139:14; James 1:22–25

E. THOUGHT TO CARRY HOME

Every person is made in God's image. Each one is valuable and worthy of redemption. But we should not take credit for who we are. We should give credit to God, who is our Creator, the Source, the Giver and Sustainer of all that we are and will become.

F. CREATIVE EXPRESSION

Paul expressed his conflict with sin in Rom. 7:22–25: "In my inner being I delight in God's law; but I see another law at work in the members of my body, waging war against the law of my mind and making me a prisoner of the law of sin at work within my members. What a wretched man I am! Who will rescue me from this body of death? Thanks be to God—through Jesus Christ our Lord!"

Write your own personalized paraphrase of these verses. Make it descriptive of what you feel right now. And don't forget the last sentence!_____
_____
_____
_____

G. SELF-EVALUATION

1. Am I delighting in the God who created me, or am I afraid to let Him see the real me?
2. Am I hiding from God? How?
3. Am I blaming others for my sin? In what ways?
4. Do I see that sin separates me from God? others?
5. What steps am I taking to deal with known sin in my life?
6. Do I read my Bible daily, let it show me who I really am?
7. Am I learning to be transparent with God? others?
8. Have I given the one who created me in His image permission to change me back into His image through a relationship with Him?

LESSON 10

UNDERSTANDING MYSELF: I AM A FREE PERSON IN CHRIST

A. DEFINITION

1. Define slavery._____
_____

2. Give a contemporary example of slavery._____

_____

3. Define freedom._____

_____

4. Give a contemporary example of freedom._____

_____

B. THINKING IT THROUGH

1. Our situation (Rom. 7:1–6)
   a. What illustration is Paul using in these verses?_____
   b. What point is he making?_____

   _____

   c. What application does this have for the Christian?_____

   _____

      1) What two kinds of "fruit" are mentioned?_____
      2) What two "ways"?_____

2. Our struggle (Rom. 7:7–24)
   a. Why were the Ten Commandments given to Israel?
   Rom. 7:7_____
   Rom. 7:12_____
   Rom. 7:13_____
   b. Count how many times the word *do* appears in Rom. 7:14–21. _____ Summarize the dilemma Paul
   describes in these verses._____

   _____

   _____

   c. Describe the two laws warring inside by picking out contrasting phrases and words from Rom. 7:6–25.

The law of God:	The law of sin:
7:6_____	_____
7:10_____	_____
7:14_____	_____
7:22, 23_____	_____
7:25_____	_____

   d. Have you experienced this frustration in your own life this week? _____ Describe your experience._____

   _____

   _____

3. Our solution (Rom. 7:25—8:39)
   a. Write the first part of Rom. 7:25—that which is preceded by an exclamation point._____

   _____

   b. What is God's purpose in sending Jesus? Rom. 8:3–4_____

   _____

   c. By whose power are we freed to live a new life? Rom. 8:5–9 _____ Describe the mind-set we
   need in order to be controlled by the Spirit._____

   _____

   d. What are the choices I can make that will free me to live according to the Spirit?_____

   _____

   _____

   e. What encouragement does God give that encourages me to make right choices for living righteously? Rom.
   8:14–17_____

   _____

Rom. 8:18–24 _____

    f. What power is available to me? Rom. 8:26–27, 34 _____

_____

  4. The triumph song (Rom. 8:28–37)

    a. This scripture passage has been entitled "More Than Conquerors" in the NIV. Note the questions Paul asks in Rom. 8:31–36 and change the *we* to *I* as you read. Write out your answers to each one.

      1) _____

      2) _____

      3) _____

      4) _____

      5) _____

      6) _____

      7) _____

C. CONTEMPORARY APPLICATION

Christian living can seem impossible at times. But it's not impossible with God.

    Ask yourself these questions to help you sort through your own struggle with sin: What am I struggling with most right now? Am I doing things that make this sin convenient? What must I avoid or put away to live righteously?

    Deciding to choose righteousness means you can live as God wants you to live: victorious in the power of the Holy Spirit. Join with Paul in the triumph song. Make music celebrating your freedom in Jesus by writing out Rom. 8:37–39 in your own words. _____

_____

_____

_____

_____

D. VERSES TO THINK ON THIS WEEK

Rom. 7:4, 24–25; Gal. 5:1, 13, 19–26

E. THOUGHT TO CARRY HOME

My only hope of overcoming sin lies in my relationship to Jesus Christ. "Thanks be to God—though Jesus Christ my Lord" (Rom. 7:25).

F. CREATIVE EXPRESSION

Do a line doodle representing the struggle Paul describes in Romans 7 and 8. Have one line represent the old nature (beware, it's crooked and twisted); the other, the new life in Jesus. Be sure to show the triumph of the Spirit.

G. SELF-EVALUATION

1. Do I recognize that triumph over sin is a process that actively involves the Holy Spirit?
2. Do I understand that growing into a mature Christian takes time? that it involves correct choices?
3. How am I further along in my Christian walk today than I was a month ago? six months? a year?
4. What failure would I rather not have on my record? Have I asked my Lord to forgive me and claimed His power to keep me from doing it again?
5. How would I describe my mind-set toward Jesus Christ? What choices am I making that reflect this?
6. How would I explain this lesson to a friend who's frustrated with sin in his life? What verse would I use to encourage him or her?

LESSON 11

UNDERSTANDING MY WORTH: I AM A WORTHY PERSON IN CHRIST

A. INTRODUCTION

"Who do you think you are?" Put down the first phrase or title that comes to your mind when you think about your relationship with Jesus Christ. "I am_____

_____

_____

_____

_____ "

(More titles and phrases are to be added as the lesson progresses.)

B. THINKING IT THROUGH

Who am I in Christ? (Eph. 1:1–14; 2:1–22; 1 Pet. 1:1—2:11)

1. Compare:

The kingdom of darkness Eph. 2:1–3	The kingdom of light Eph. 2:4–10; 1 Pet. 2:9
_____	_____
_____	_____
_____	_____
_____	_____

   "God . . . called you out of darkness into His wonderful light" (1 Pet. 2:9b).

2. Read Ephesians 1 and add descriptive words and titles to your introductory statement above. As you select, also count the number of times the word *in* is used in connection with Jesus Christ. How many did you find? _____ . Finish this sentence: "I am a worthy person _____ Christ because . . .

3. He created me. (Gen. 1:26–27; 2:7)

   a. Why is it important to believe that I am created by God and didn't evolve from an ape?_____

   _____

   b. How has God created me twice? (2 Cor. 5:17; Eph. 2:8–10; Col. 3:9–10)_____

   _____

4. He saved me.

   a. What was God's purpose in providing for my salvation? (John 3:16; Gal. 5:13; Eph. 2:10)_____

   _____

   b. Why does God have a valid claim on my life?_____

   _____

5. He indwells me. (Eph. 1:13–14)

   a. How does He equip me to live for Him?_____

   _____

   b. What is the symbol of the Holy Spirit's guarantee that He is equipping me as His possession?_____

   c. What is the purpose of His seal?

   Eph 1:14_____

   Eph. 2:10_____

6. He perfects me.
   a. What are two of God's objectives in saving me?
      Eph. 1:12_____
      2 Cor. 3:18_____
   b. What does He want me to do with my life? (1 Pet. 2:11–12)_____
      _____
      _____
   c. What is God's timetable for this plan? (Isa. 55:8; 2 Pet. 3:8–9)_____
      _____
      _____
   d. What are the ultimate results? (Phil. 1:6; Rev. 21:1–3)_____
      _____
      _____

7. Because I am His creation, saved by His blood, indwelt by His Spirit, and perfected by His work, I represent Jesus to those around me.
   a. Acts 8:30, 35. Philip represented Jesus to_____
   b. Acts 16:29–30. Paul and Silas to_____
   c. Acts 18:26. Priscilla and Aquila to_____
   d. Acts 26:27–29. Paul to_____
   e. Acts 9:36, 39. Dorcas to_____

C. CONTEMPORARY APPLICATION

Take a mental walk through your day tomorrow. Whom will you meet? Is there someone in one of your classes who needs to know how to come from the dark kingdom into the light? Or is that person in the darkness someone in your own family?

How can you represent Jesus to that one?

D. VERSES TO THINK ON THIS WEEK

2 Cor. 3:2–3; Eph. 1:13–14, 18–20; Eph. 2:10

E. THOUGHT TO CARRY HOME

I can do all things "in Christ." He doesn't leave me to do things alone but empowers and equips me for good works.

F. CREATIVE EXPRESSION

Pick out one of the titles you bear as a believer and write and/or design a bumper sticker. Include the phrase *in Christ.*

OR

Liken yourself to the living letter Paul describes in 2 Cor. 3:2–3. Letters in those days were sealed with a special seal that bore the mark of the sender. Eph. 1:13 says we are sealed with the Holy Spirit as a pledge of God's working in us, guaranteeing us our complete redemption. Design a seal representing His Spirit in the space below.

G. SELF-EVALUATION

1. Which qualities do I reflect most in my life? those of darkness or those of light?
2. How would I describe the results of my being God's workmanship?
3. Who comes into my mind when I'm reminded I represent Jesus to someone?
4. Am I willing to show light to that person by putting aside the works of darkness?
5. Am I willing to ask God to help me live as a child of the King before them?

LESSON 12

UNDERSTANDING MY NEED: I AM A POWERFUL PERSON IN CHRIST

A. DEFINITION

Define "spiritual power" by breaking it into two parts.

1. spiritual_____
2. power_____
3. Combine the terms into one or two simple phrases or sentences._____
_____

B. THINKING IT THROUGH

We inherit spiritual power through a personal relationship with Jesus Christ. But certain prerequisites are necessary to activate this power and make it evident in our lives.

1. We will be spiritually powerful if we know God.
   a. List people you've known that you think have or had great spiritual power. _____ , _____ ,
   _____ , _____ , _____ , _____ , _____ .
   Do you think you can ever be like them? Why or why not?_____
   _____
   _____
   b. What power is given to us when we know God?
   Matt. 28:18_____
   Acts 1:8_____
   c. How do we get to know God?
   John 15:4_____
   Heb. 4:12_____
   d. How is our relationship to God's Son, Jesus Christ, revealed in the following verses?
   1 Cor. 2:16_____
   1 Cor. 3:23_____
   Eph. 1:18–23_____
   Phil. 2:9–11_____
2. We will be spiritually powerful if we avoid sin.
   a. What happens if you plug in a lamp, then cut the cord?_____
   _____
   b. Sin cuts off our power source. How, then, can I avoid it? (Gal. 5:16–18)_____
   c. What must I sometimes do to avoid sin? (2 Tim. 2:22)_____
   _____

    d. What promises has God given to those who are upright and pure in heart?
       Prov. 3:32_____
       Matt. 5:8_____

    e. Jesus' own blood paid the price for my sins (1 Pet. 1:18–19). I can claim its power to equip me with what?
       (Heb. 13:20–21)_____
       _____

3. We will be spiritually powerful if we see our inadequacy.
    a. How does God see us? Ps. 103:14–16_____
    b. What do you think Jesus meant when He talked about the ''the poor in spirit? Matt. 5:3_____
       _____
    c. What did Paul learn from his weaknesses? 2 Cor. 12:9–10_____
    d. What did he say was the true source of his power? Phil. 4:13_____
       _____
    e. Realizing Jesus is my source of strength enables me to bear what? John 15:4–5_____
    f. According to Gal. 5:22–23, this is shown in my life through . . ._____
       _____

4. We will be spiritually powerful if we recognize our enemy.
    a. Satan is real, but not human. Still, he has some characteristics of a person. He can . . .
       Isa. 14:13_____
       Isa. 14:13–14_____
       Rev. 12:12_____
    b. He is described in 1 Pet. 5:8 as a_____
       _____
    c. Is Jesus' power greater than Satan's? 1 John 4:4_____
    d. How has he been defeated? Col. 2:13–15_____
    e. Why am I incapable of spiritual victory without Christ? 2 Cor. 10:3–6_____
       _____
    f. List the armor God provides for our safety and victory. Eph. 6:10–20.
       _____
       _____
       _____
       _____
       _____
       _____
       _____

PUT ON THE FULL ARMOR OF GOD SO YOU CAN STAND UP TO ANYTHING!

C. CONTEMPORARY APPLICATION

There are good and bad examples of spiritual power all around us. What have you seen concerning it? What have you heard about it in the news? Have you talked about it with your friends? Do you think some people are in touch with evil power? Have you ever experienced fear just hearing about it?

God's power of righteousness and freedom is far more powerful than the powers of darkness. This power is available to us the moment we become His children, and we can experience it in our lives if we depend on Him.

D. VERSES TO THINK ON THIS WEEK

2 Cor. 10:3–6; Eph. 6:10; 2 Pet. 1:3–4

E. THOUGHT TO CARRY HOME

Through God's strength, I can be a powerful person for His kingdom.

F. CREATIVE EXPRESSION

Draw a simple sketch of the full armor of God described in Ephesians 6. Label each part.

Write a prayer thanking God for providing the right kind of covering to make you an able soldier, battling in the King's army. Then respond to Eph. 6:18–20 by praying for the family of God.

G. SELF-EVALUATION

1. Do I feel I am being controlled by sin and Satan rather than Jesus Christ? If I am, what am I going to do about it?
2. What steps am I taking to get to know God better?
3. What actions am I taking to avoid sin?
4. What areas of personal weakness do I see in my life? Am I allowing them to draw me closer to God? Do I depend more fully upon His strength?
5. What do I see happening in my life that I can attribute to the power of the Holy Spirit?

LESSON 13

UNDERSTANDING MY INNER ATTRACTIVENESS: I AM AN APPEALING PERSON IN CHRIST

A. DEFINITION

1. What pictures or symbols would you use to represent the words *holy, purity*?_____

2. What pictures or symbols would you use to represent the words *unholy, impurity*?_____

3. What colors or concepts suggest holiness?_____

4. What colors or concepts suggest unholiness?_____

5. List some synonyms and antonyms for the words *holy* and *pure*.
   Synonyms:_____
   Antonyms:_____
6. What is character?_____

B. THINKING IT THROUGH

1. The real you: inside or outside?
   a. Does most of today's advertising focus on the outside or the inside of a person?_____
   _____

   b. Compare how God sees with how man sees. (1 Sam. 16:7; 1 Pet. 3:3–5)_____
   _____
   _____

   c. What does Jesus say about the inside versus the outside? (Mark 7:14–23)_____
   _____

   d. In Scripture the word *heart* means mind, soul, spirit, emotions, personality—what's really you inside. Personalize meaningful concepts from the following verses by rewriting them, using first person (I, me, my, etc.): Deut. 6:5; Jer. 17:9; Mark 7:20–23; Ps. 51:2, 10; Isa. 61:1:_____
   _____
   _____
   _____
   _____
   _____
   _____
   _____

   e. Respond to this statement: If we want to be outwardly appealing, we must first cultivate inward appeal (2 Cor. 3:18; 1 Pet. 3:3–5). Do you agree or disagree? Describe a truly attractive person._____
   _____
   _____

2. The real issue: our Holy God demands holiness. (Lev. 20:7; 1 Pet. 1:13—2:1)
   a. What is the relationship between God and holiness? (Isa. 6:3; Rev. 15:4)_____
   _____

   b. Between us and holiness? (Rom. 6:19, 22; Eph. 1:4; Titus 1:15; 1 Pet. 1:15)_____
   _____
   _____

   c. Personal holiness is a work of gradual development. How does it become a part of our lives? (1 Cor. 1:30; 2 Cor. 7:1; Eph. 4:23–24)_____
   _____
   _____

   d. Can we truly know God apart from pursuing His holiness?_____
   _____

   SIN KEEPS US FROM KNOWING GOD BECAUSE HOLINESS IS THE HEART OF GOD.

3. The real dilemma: living holy lives in an unholy world.
   a. Respond to the statement: There is no true attractiveness apart from true holiness. Agree or disagree? What do the following verses in the King James Version say about beauty and holiness?
   1 Chron. 16:29_____
   Ps. 29:2_____
   Ps. 96:9_____
   b. What *effect* does personal holiness have on our total person?
   1) Mentally:
   Phil. 4:8_____
   Rom. 12:2_____
   2 Cor. 10:4, 5_____
   2) Emotionally:
   Eph. 4:26–27_____

Prov. 14:30 KJV_____

Dan. 5:19–21_____

3) Physically:

1 Thess. 4:1–8_____

1 Cor. 6:15–20_____

1 Cor. 11:28–30_____

Personal holiness is an act of obedience. As we cultivate holiness in our lives, it affects our daily personal choices and behavior (Col. 3:12).

C. CONTEMPORARY APPLICATION

Holiness is unpopular in our day. It is seen as old-fashioned. To be contemporary some people say we must be progressive, open-minded, flexible. But these attitudes are often excuses for personal sin.

God has designed holiness for our benefit and our attractiveness. Because He has, we can feel confident in our right choices and godly behavior.

D. VERSES TO THINK ON THIS WEEK

Lev. 19:2; Ps. 99:3–5; Prov. 9:10; Col. 3:12

E. THOUGHT TO CARRY HOME

"True beauty comes from true holiness. True holiness comes from our close walk with our holy God."

F. CREATIVE EXPRESSION

List key words which give spiritual significance to the clothing or jewelry mentioned in the following verses.

1. Isa. 61:10a _____ , _____

2. Rev. 19:7–8 _____ _____

3. Prov. 1:8–9 _____ _____ , _____ _____

4. Prov. 3:3 _____ and _____

5. Prov. 3:21–22 _____ _____ , _____

Put a star beside the one which you would like to have be more visible in your life. Write a brief sentence explaining why you chose that particular one._____

_____

G. SELF-EVALUATION

1. How do my actions reveal what I believe about God's holiness?

2. How am I being made attractive inside?

3. What am I doing to cultivate this inward appeal?

4. Is practical holiness instant or progressive? Is personal holiness realistic for me?

5. What are some specific ways I can live a holy life in an unholy world?

6. What do my choices reveal about my character?

SECTION III

SEEING MY POTENTIAL: MODELS OF GODLY MEN AND WOMEN

"Therefore, since we are surrounded by such a great cloud of witnesses . . ."
(Heb. 12:1).

Section Objective: To see our potential as modeled in the lives of godly men and women.

LESSON 14

ABRAHAM, A MAN OF FEAR AND FAITH

A. INTRODUCTION

Do a time line for the life of Abraham by marking off chapters 11–25 and writing in events.

1. Write a brief description of Abraham's character._____

2. What do you most remember him for?_____

B. THINKING IT THROUGH

Abraham's early walk with God was characterized by fearfulness, yet he is remembered for his faithfulness. Note his personal growth in these verses and write down what you think might be symptoms of fear.

1. Fearfulness
   a. Gen. 11:31—12:5_____

   b. Gen. 12:10–20_____

   c. Gen. 16_____

   d. Gen. 20_____

2. Faithfulness:
   Be observant of how God reveals himself to Abraham and how Abraham grows in his awareness of who God is. Note his growth into a man of faith.

a. Gen. 12:1–9. How do we see faith demonstrated in Abraham's life in this instance?_____
_____

b. Gen. 15:1–6. Abraham addresses God as *Adonai* (Master or Lord, translated Sovereign LORD in the NIV). What does this show you about how Abraham perceives His God? (Turn to Lesson 6 for additional help.)
_____
_____

c. Gen. 17:1–8, 15–21. God reveals himself for the first time as *El Shaddai*—the All-Sufficient One, the Almighty God. How does this show how Abraham perceives his God? (Review truth from Lesson 4.)____
_____

List the specifics of God's promise._____
_____
_____
_____

3. Gen. 22:1–19. God reveals himself to Abraham with a new name: *Jehovah-Jirah*, the Lord will Provide.

a. Read verses 1–3. Try to imagine how Abraham felt when he heard these words. Write a description of what you think his feelings were._____
_____
_____

b. Write a description of how you would feel if God asked you to give up the most important person in your life: your best friend, your girlfriend or boyfriend, a parent, favorite uncle, etc._____
_____
_____

c. Gen. 22:14. When Abraham says, "The Lord will provide . . . On the mountain of the LORD it will be provided," he is looking to Calvary, the scene of that grand and awful sacrifice of God's only Son, Jesus Christ, the righteous, sinless one.

   1) Read John 8:56. Do you think Abraham might have had more understanding than we realize? _____
      Why or why not?_____

   2) To Abraham God revealed the awful cost to himself of providing His Son, His only Son, as a sacrifice for sin. The thing Abraham foreshadowed on Mount Moriah was realized when God's Son, nailed to the cross, cried out, " _____ _____ _____ " (John 19:30).

   3) God himself provided the sacrifice. In the mount of the Lord He was seen, the Savior, the _____ who takes away the sin of the world (John 1:29; 1 Pet. 1:18–19; Rev. 5:11–13).

4. We sometimes focus on Abraham's fearfulness instead of his faithfulness. Yet over and over God calls Him a man of faith. What do these New Testament verses say about Abraham's faithfulness?

   a. Rom. 4:19–22_____

   b. Gal. 3:6_____

   c. Heb. 11:8, 17_____

   d. James 2:23_____

C. CONTEMPORARY APPLICATION

What speaks to you about Abraham's fearfulness? his faithfulness? Summarize what you feel is the most important lesson for you to take away from this study._____
_____
_____
_____

D. VERSES TO MEMORIZE THIS WEEK

Heb. 11:1–2: "Now faith is being sure of what we hope for and certain of what we do not see. This is what the ancients were commended for."

E. THOUGHT TO CARRY HOME

In the New Testament, Abraham's faithfulness, not his fearfulness, is highlighted. This teaches me that God can use me right where I am, no matter how insignificant I think I might be.

F. CREATIVE EXPRESSION

How would you describe Abraham if you were given the job of writing his epitaph? (An epitaph is an inscription on a tomb, or a short composition in prose or verse, written as a tribute to a dead person.) For thought starters, review the New Testament verses to see how those writers described Abraham._____

_____

_____

Now write an epitaph for yourself. How do you want people to remember you?_____

_____

G. SELF-EVALUATION

1. Are there areas in my life which I am afraid to entrust to God? Would I dare to trust and obey Him even if some things didn't make sense?

2. Do I have the courage to trust His promises even though years may pass before they're fulfilled?

3. Am I beginning to trust God more through understanding His names?

4. Am I beginning to see that even though I may be in a position of what I thought was useless fearfulness, God can still use me? Am I trusting God even when I can't see how the pieces of my life fit together?

5. In what areas in my life am I moving from fearfulness to faithfulness?

6. Do I see how God used Abraham's unique personality to impact his world?

7. Do I see how God can use me (even with my weaknesses) to change my world? Do I want God to make me into a person of faith?

LESSON 15

JACOB, A MAN WHO TRIED TO MAKE IT ON HIS OWN

A. INTRODUCTION

1. What do you think is the difference between a self-dependent person and a God-dependent person?_____

_____

2. Why is it so hard for some people to trust God?_____

_____

3. Why is it sometimes hard for you to trust Him?_____

_____

B. THINKING IT THROUGH

1. Jacob's heritage (Gen. 11:31; 21:1–3; 24:67; 25:19–26)

   a. Do you think it is easier to trust God if a person has had Christian heritage? (Dad and Mom both strong Christians, active in church work, etc.) _____

   b. Examine the following verses and write down what Jacob's heritage was like. Who were his grandparents? (Gen. 11:31; 21:1–3) _____. Who were his parents? (Gen. 24:67; 25:19–26) _____. What do you remember about them? What were they like? (See Heb. 11:8–12, 17–20; Gen. 24:1.)

strengths	weaknesses
_____	_____
_____	_____
_____	_____

   c. What promises did God make to the men in the families?
      Abraham: Gen. 12:1–3; 13:14–17; 15:1–6, 18; 17:1–8_____

      _____

Isaac: Gen. 26:2–5, 24_____

_____

d. What particular sin do we find in Jacob's family tree?
   Abraham: Gen. 12:10–20; 20:1–13_____
   Isaac: Gen. 26:7–11_____

e. Look at your own heritage. What strengths and weaknesses do you see?

strengths	weaknesses
_____	_____
_____	_____
_____	_____

2. The deceit marking Jacob's early years.
   a. Write on the signposts below the incidents that illustrate Jacob's deceitful ways.

Gen. 25:26   **Gen. 25:27–34**   **Gen. 27:1–40**

   b. Explain how the last event affected Esau's relationship with Jacob. Gen. 27:41–45_____

_____

3. Jacob's crisis and his encounters with God.
   a. Encounter #1: Jacob hears from God. (Gen. 28:10–22)
      1) Where is Jacob going and why? (Gen. 27:41–45; 28:10)_____

_____

      2) What does God tell Jacob in his dream? (Gen. 28:13–15) Paraphrase it in your own words._____

_____

      Paraphrase Jacob's response. (Gen. 28:20–22)_____

_____

_____

      Personalize Jacob's response by answering these questions:
      a) Have I ever made a conditional promise to God? _____
      b) Have I followed through with it? _____
      c) Does Gen. 31:20–21 indicate that Jacob hadn't really changed, that he's still doing what he wants
         to do *in his own way* instead of God's? Why or why not?_____

_____

      d) How is this further indicated as he plans to meet his brother, Esau, in Gen. 32:3–21?_____

_____

   b. Encounter #2: Jacob wrestles with God. (Gen. 32:24–32)
      1) Jacob's stubborn independence is here tested by God in a hard-to-understand wrestling match resulting
         in a change in his _____ (32:31) and a change in his _____ (32:31). God had to
         touch Jacob with physical weakness before he would come to the place of trusting God and His power.

4. Jacob's later years. (Gen. 35:1–15)

a. Note the changes in Jacob's life since the first time God appeared to him in Bethel. Then Jacob was fearful; now he is f _____ . Then he was running; now he is r _____ . Then he was compromising; now he is c _____ .

b. What do these verses say about Jacob's faith in his old age?
Gen. 46:1–4_____
Gen. 48:3, 4_____
Gen 48:15, 16, 20, Heb. 11:21_____
_____

C. CONTEMPORARY APPLICATION

What part of Jacob's life is most like yours? Do you deal with a recurring sin or trait in your family tree? Do you struggle with submitting yourself totally to God?

D. VERSES TO MEMORIZE THIS WEEK

1 Pet. 5:5b, 6: "God opposes the proud but gives grace to the humble. Humble yourselves therefore, under God's mighty hand, that he may lift you up in due time."

E. THOUGHT TO CARRY HOME

God will not force us into a relationship with himself. But He may order circumstances so we have nowhere to turn but to Him.

F. CREATIVE EXPRESSION

Think back over your own life and make several signposts. Write in significant incidents and circumstances on each. Ask yourself who was in control of each circumstance—self or God. Put the answer beneath each one. As you think and draw, ask yourself, "Whom do I really want to be in charge here?"

G. SELF-EVALUATION

1. When I'm in a crisis, do I try to work it out myself or do I turn to God?
2. Do I know that God wants me to trust Him in all things?
3. Do I believe that God is powerful enough and interested enough to control all things, even me?
4. Have I ever been like Jacob and tried to use God as an emergency exit out of a pressing problem?
5. Have I made promises to God that I haven't kept?
6. If God allowed me to experience a physical injury in an effort to teach me I must depend on Him, would I trust Him?

LESSON 16

JOSEPH, A MAN WHO REFUSED TO COMPROMISE

A. INTRODUCTION

1. Define compromise._____
_____
_____

B. THINKING IT THROUGH

You may think Joseph's life has little relevance to you today. But the experiences Joseph went through can teach lessons about choices we face daily.

The following chart deals with seven significant events in Joseph's life. Discern the event from the scripture given, look at Joseph's possible responses and then make the application to your own situation.

ACTION	ATTITUDE	APPLICATION
1._____ (Gen. 37:18–28)	forgiveness resentment	_____ _____
2._____ (Gen. 39:5–10)	resist sin give in	_____ _____
3._____ (Gen. 39:11–19)	God in control bitterness	_____ _____
4._____ (Gen. 39:19–23)	contentment resentment	_____ _____
5._____ (Gen. 40:1–4, 20, 23)	trust hostility	_____ _____
6._____ (Gen. 41:1–8, 14–16)	humility pride	_____ _____
7._____ (Gen. 42:1–8; 45:1–7)	forgiveness revenge	_____ _____

C. CONTEMPORARY APPLICATION

Choose the attitude you feel you need most to cultivate in order to grow into an uncompromising Christian.____

What specifically can you do this week that reflects your choice?_____

How do you expect your life to be different because of your decision?_____

D. VERSES TO MEMORIZE THIS WEEK

Rom. 8:31–32: "What then shall we say in response to this? If God is for us, who can be against us? He who did not spare his own Son, but gave him up for us all—how will he not also, along with him, graciously give us all things?"

E. THOUGHT TO CARRY HOME

Joseph was in a position to get his own way a number of times, but he considered his commitment to God too great a thing to compromise. Joseph accepted God as sovereign in every detail of his life.

F. CREATIVE EXPRESSION

Write a story (by yourself or with another student), imagining what events might have taken place if Joseph had chosen to compromise in one of the areas from 1 to 7. Choose the one you most identify with.____

_____

G. SELF-EVALUATION

1. How do I react when I'm mistreated?
2. How do I react when I'm morally tempted?
3. How do I react when I'm misunderstood?
4. How do I react when I'm treated unfairly?
5. How do I react when I'm greatly disappointed?
6. How do I react when I've accomplished something great?
7. How do I react when I meet those I personally dislike?

LESSON 17

NAOMI, A WOMAN WHO TOOK HER EYES OFF GOD

A. INTRODUCTION

1. Judges is the setting for the Book of Ruth. A good verse to describe the times is Judg. 17:6. Look it up in the KJV and write it here._____

_____

  a. According to this description, what kind of problems might the Israelites have been facing?_____

_____

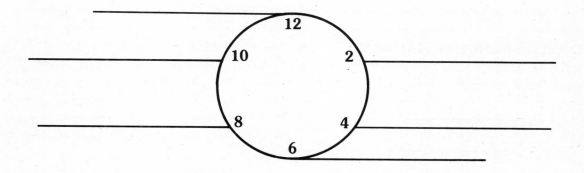

Because of sin, Israel repeatedly experienced the "Judges cycle." Write "rebellion" at 6; "discipline" at 8; "cry for deliverance" at 10; "God answers" at 12; "repentance" at 2; "restoration" at 4. This cycle occurs and reoccurs throughout the Book of Judges.

Where would you place the Book of Ruth in this circle? Clue: Famine has been used by God as a discipline to bring His people back to himself (Jer. 16:4, 10–11; Ruth 1:1). Add the word *Ruth* to the judges cycle.

B. THINKING IT THROUGH

1. Describe the tragedy in Naomi's life. (Ruth 1:1–5)_____

_____

  What are her needs?
  Physical_____

  Emotional_____

  Spiritual_____

2. How does she describe her life?
   a. To Ruth? (1:13)_____
   b. To the women at the well? (1:20)_____

3. Read Heb. 12:5–15 and pick out words that describe the hard part of God's discipline in the Christian's life.

   _____

4. Look for God's purpose in disciplining His children. What does He desire in our lives?
   a. 12:10_____
   b. 12:11_____
   c. 12:12_____
   d. 12:13_____
   e. 12:14_____
   f. 12:15_____

5. Write down your definition of bitterness. Compare it with the dictionary definition._____

   _____
   _____
   _____

6. What word is used to describe bitter water in Ex. 15:23–25?_____
   Compare it with what Naomi asked the women to call her in Ruth 1:20.
   What do the verses in Exodus show us about God's power?_____

7. Heb. 12:11 is descriptive of Naomi's life as she went from a place of hopelessness and bitterness (Ruth 1:11) to a place of healing and usefulness. Write it here._____

   _____
   _____

8. Even though Naomi is struggling with negatives (bitterness and self pity), she is very aware of God. Notice how often His name is on her lips in Ruth 1:9, 13, 21–22: What does she call Him in each verse?
   a. 1:9_____
   b. 1:13, 21_____
   c. 1:21, 22_____

9. Ruth 2 and 3 reveal Naomi's spiritual growth. Match the following character strengths of Naomi with the corresponding scripture references. Naomi is shown as

1) an encourager	Ruth 3:16–17
2) thankful	Ruth 2:20
3) a protector	Ruth 3:18
4) a counselor	Ruth 3:4
5) interested in others	Ruth 2:2
6) a wise person	Ruth 2:21–22

10. Which characteristic do you most desire to have evident in your life?_____

   _____

   Consider what step you can take this week to help you grow in that area. Write it down._____

   _____

11. Read Ruth 4:14–17. Compare the words describing Naomi in 1:5 to what the women say in 4:14. Discover the "sound-alike phrases" and write them down._____

   _____
   _____

12. Explain how Heb. 12:11 could be the theme verse for Naomi's life._____

_____

_____

C. CONTEMPORARY APPLICATION

How do you react to discipline? What is your attitude when you receive bad grades at school and your parents discipline you by taking away your telephone privileges or car keys? Do you struggle with a bitter root of rebellion, anger? Or do you accept the discipline with an uncomplaining spirit that results in better grades and a happier home?

D. VERSE TO MEMORIZE THIS WEEK

Heb. 12:11: "No discipline seems pleasant at the time, but painful. Later on, however, it produces a harvest of righteousness and peace for those who have been trained by it."

E. THOUGHT TO CARRY HOME

Bitter roots keep spiritual fruit from forming in our lives. Review the fruit of the Spirit (Gal. 5:22–23), and ask God what He would have you cultivate this week.

F. CREATIVE EXPRESSION

Draw a picture of what you imagine a bitter root would look like,

    OR

Draw a tree (Ps. 1) bearing the fruit of the Spirit (Gal. 5:22–23). Label the fruit as given in Galatians. Label the leaves with the strong qualities you discovered in Naomi's life.

G. SELF-EVALUATION

1. Do I desire spiritual growth in my life?
2. What is my attitude toward discipline?
3. Am I hindering God's working in my life by nurturing a bitter root?
4. Am I willing to let Him root it out, even though the uprooting causes pain?
5. Am I trusting His power to transform it into a sweetness that will enhance my life and the lives of others?
6. With which of Naomi's strong character qualities do I most identify?
7. What about her weaknesses? What have I learned from them?
8. Am I willing to be honest with God when He disciplines me from His Word?
9. What has God said to me today that I need to heed in order to develop into a stronger person?

LESSON 18

RUTH, A BEAUTIFUL WOMAN WHO MAKES THE RIGHT DECISION

A. INTRODUCTION

Locate the country of Moab in either the map section of a study Bible or in a Bible Atlas. Note its proximity to Judah, the home of the Israelites. Find the city of Bethlehem.

Background information: Moab was Israel's enemy, an idolatrous nation of unfriendly, hostile people. Ruth is like an oasis in this sinful land; even her name means "beauty" and "appearance," the root word being "to feed a flock."

1. Write down the contrasts in Isa. 61:3 (KJV)._____

_____

_____

2. Contrast the adjectives and nouns that describe Moab and Ruth in the above background information:

          Moab   Ruth

   _____   _____

   _____   _____

   _____   _____

B. THINKING IT THROUGH

Ruth's Choice (Ruth 1; 2:12)

1. Put yourself in Ruth's sandals in chapter 1. What do you see?_____
_____

What do you feel?_____
What emotions probably prompted her words in 1:16–17?_____
_____

2. What do Naomi's words in 1:15 reveal about the significance of Ruth's decision? (Clue: Note what Orpah went back to.)_____
_____

3. Closely examine Ruth's words (Ruth 1:16–17).
   a. What six things did Ruth intend to do?
   1) _____
   2) _____
   3) _____
   4) _____
   5) _____
   6) _____
   b. Put a star beside the one which you think is the most important. Write down your reason for choosing it.
   _____
   _____

4. How is Ruth's relationship to God described in Ruth 2:12?_____
_____

5. Examine Ruth's words and actions in the following verses. Look for strong character qualities that you can emulate:
   a. Ruth 2:2–4, 6–7, 14–15, 17_____
   b. Ruth 2:10–13_____
   c. Ruth 2:18–23_____

6. Note the background information. How does Ruth's name reveal her character?_____
_____

7. Each of us has a circle of influence. Ruth had a very good reputation. What did others notice about her life?
   a. Boaz (Ruth 3:10–11)_____
   b. Boaz's employees (2:6, 7)_____
   c. The townspeople (2:11)_____

8. Choose a character quality from Ruth's life that you'd like to develop in your own life. _____ Write a prayer asking God to help you in your area of need._____
_____
_____

9. What was Ruth's reward? (Ruth 4)_____
_____
_____

   a. What blessing did the women speak to Boaz? (4:11–12)_____
   _____

b. What was their prophetic fulfillment? (Mic. 5:2; Matt. 1:5; Luke 2:10–11)_____
_____

c. How did the women characterize Ruth when they spoke to Naomi? (Ruth 4:15)_____
_____

10. Ruth's rewards came as a result of her choice in Ruth 1:16–17 and 2:12. However, her choice was actually twofold: she chose Naomi's God while living with Naomi in Moab, but she made her total commitment while on the road to Bethlehem. Are our choices ever twofold? _____
  a. Prayerfully examine Rom. 12:1–2 and note the choice before each person who makes a decision to follow Christ. What is God asking each of us to do?_____
_____
  b. Write down the choice you have made or want to make now._____
_____
  c. Compare your choice to Ruth's._____
_____

11. The ultimate reward for placing our trust in Jesus Christ is heaven. What do you like best about God's description in Rev. 21:1–4?_____
_____

  Why?_____

C. CONTEMPORARY APPLICATION

Ruth chose the best in her relationship with God, with Naomi, and with Boaz, and she was rewarded. What choices can you make to help you have the best relationship possible with others? How will it be rewarded?

D. VERSE TO MEMORIZE THIS WEEK

Psalm 91:4: "He will cover you with his feathers, and under his wings you will find refuge; his faithfulness will be your shield and rampart."

E. THOUGHT TO CARRY HOME

Placing our complete trust in our God is the first step in developing a strong character that honors Jesus Christ.

F. CREATIVE EXPRESSION

Draw a winged creature: eagle, or a bird of your choice. Underneath your drawing write Ps. 91:4, "Under His wings you will find refuge," and claim it for your own by writing your name for *you*, Jesus for *His*.

G. SELF-EVALUATION

1. What difference did Ruth's knowing God as her refuge make in her life?
2. Am I willing to accept the protection of God's wings? Or am I trying to fly solo?
3. Has Ruth's choice shown me an action that I need to take?
4. Have I made the same twofold choice that she did?
5. Have I accepted God as my refuge and strength? If I have, what character strengths am I developing?
6. Am I learning to think of others and their needs? What am I doing this week that demonstrates my willingness to consider others?

LESSON 19

BOAZ, A MAN WHO HAD IT ALL TOGETHER

A. INTRODUCTION

Every year at harvest the Midianites swept into Israel under cover of darkness and plundered their harvest. The Israelites were even driven into caves and rocks.

Boaz knew what it meant to need a refuge. Where is your place of refuge when you want to get away from people and pressures?_____

Draw a refuge (a place of protection, strong tower, fortress, rock). Put yourself in it.

B. THINKING IT THROUGH

1. What strong character qualities do you see in Boaz's life?
   Ruth 2:8–9_____
   2:11–12_____
   2:14–17, 20; 3:15–17_____
   3:12–14_____
   4:1–9_____

2. How do others see Boaz?
   a. His employees? (Ruth 2:1–9, 15–17)_____
   _____

   b. Naomi? (Ruth 2:19—3:4)_____
   _____

   c. Ruth? (Ruth 3:13–18)_____
   _____

3. Try to identify with how Boaz feels about himself. Step into his sandals. Night is falling, and he's thinking about what to write in his journal. He has finished eating and drinking and is in good spirits (see Ruth 3:7) as he crawls under his wool blanket. He begins to write:_____
   _____
   _____
   _____
   _____

4. How does Boaz see God? (Ruth 2:12)_____

   a. Respond to this quote: "The most important thing about me is what I believe about God."—A. W. Tozer
   I agree, disagree, or somewhere in-between. Why?_____
   _____

b. The way a person understands God is revealed by his behavior. Because Boaz had claimed God as his refuge, he was able to give refuge to Ruth. Think over what you've studied, then write a sentence that tells what specific actions Boaz took to become a refuge for Ruth. If you need help, look back at Ruth 2:8–18; 3:7–15; 4:1–10, 13._____

_____

_____

_____

C. CONTEMPORARY APPLICATION

God wants us to share tangibly with others. Are there those in your community who need the basic necessities of life: food and shelter? Do you think God wants to use the church to help meet their needs? What is your church doing in this area? What should be our motivation for helping?

D. VERSE TO MEMORIZE THIS WEEK

Isa. 32:2: "Each man will be like a shelter from the wind and a refuge from the storm, like streams of water in the desert and the shadow of a great rock in a thirsty land."

E. THOUGHT TO CARRY HOME

The way I see God transforms my behavior in practical ways. Boaz's strong belief that God was His refuge enabled him to share with Ruth not only his convictions about who God was, but his own actions expressed that truth in practical ways.

F. CREATIVE EXPRESSION

Write your own personal psalm to God, your refuge. Read Ps. 31:1–5 to stimulate your creativity._____

_____

_____

_____

G. SELF-EVALUATION

1. Which of Boaz's character strengths is most evident in my life?
2. How is this strength shown to others? to myself?
3. What character quality does Boaz have that I lack?
4. How can I develop it in my own life?
5. Am I looking for ways in which God can reveal himself to me?
6. Does understanding that God is my refuge make me feel good about my God? about myself?
7. How can knowing God as my refuge change my actions and develop strong character qualities in my life?
8. What character qualities do I need to develop in order to become a refuge to someone in need?
9. Am I willing to ask God to show me someone to whom I can offer my support or protection this week?
10. In what ways can I go beyond what's expected of me?

LESSON 20

HANNAH, A WOMAN OF COMMITMENT AND JOY

A. INTRODUCTION

Hannah's story is the bridge suspended between the era of the judges and the era ushered in by the kings. Her life shines as a pageant of praise to the God she worshiped and served.

B. THINKING IT THROUGH: A Prayer, a Cry, and a Song (1 Samuel 1, 2)

1. Contrast the two women who were wives of Elkanah as described in 1 Sam. 1:2._____

_____

2. How does Elkanah express his feelings for Hannah?_____

_____

3. Carefully observe 1 Sam. 1:6–10 and pick out words that describe how Hannah felt._____

_____

What two things made Hannah feel this way?_____

_____

4. Where does Hannah go to pray? (v. 9)_____
   a. Hannah's prayer (1 Sam. 1:11).
     The original words translated LORD Almighty are *Jehovah Sabaoth*, which means, Lord of hosts. It is the name of the LORD in manifestation of power. As LORD of hosts, God is able to gather all the hosts of earth and heaven to help His people.
     1) Why do you think Hannah addresses her God by this name?_____

             _____

     2) What does she ask for? _____ What does she tell God she'll do if He answers her request?_____

     3) What is Eli's reaction to her as she's praying?_____

             _____

     4) How does Hannah explain her feelings and what she's doing?_____

             _____

     5) How does Eli respond?_____

             _____

     6) What change is there in Hannah that reveals her trust in God's answer? (Compare 1:7b with 1:18b.)

             _____

   b. Your prayer.
     Have you experienced or are you experiencing pain inside that has you in the pits? Is there anything that is bothering you in your relationship with God or someone else? God desires that you release this situation or hurt to Him; tell Him every intimate detail. Write a personal prayer to God expressing the need in your heart. Address it to the Lord of hosts, the powerful God, able to help us with any need. (Heb. 2:16)____

             _____

             _____

             _____

   c. God's answer.
     1) How did God answer Hannah's prayer?_____

     2) How is she shown as a woman of commitment in 1 Sam. 1:21–28? Summarize Elkanah and Hannah's actions:_____

             _____

5. Do a comparison study on the prayer Hannah sang when she gave Samuel to her Lord, and Mary's song commonly called the "Magnificat." Mary echoes many of Hannah's words. Discover for yourself how the praises of these two women reveal their knowledge of God.
   a. Compare the first sentence of each of the woman's song:
   Hannah (1 Sam. 2:1–10)   Mary (Luke 1:46–55)

   _____   _____

   b. Pick out words that emphasize God's attributes and identity.
     Finish the sentences:

Hannah sees God as . . .   Mary sees God as . . .

her strong deliverer_____   _____

_____   _____

_____   _____

_____   _____

_____   _____

_____   _____

_____   _____

_____   _____

_____   _____

_____   _____

_____   _____

_____

c. Both women recognized God's sovereignty, that God is in complete control of the universe and of the unseen hosts of heaven and earth. Examine Luke 1:46–55 and 1 Sam. 2:6–10. What similarities do you see between Hannah and Mary's words?_____

_____

_____

d. When both women released everything into God's hands, they experienced a new dimension in trust that found expression in joy. What area of your life do you need to trust to God's sovereignty?_____

_____

_____

C. CONTEMPORARY APPLICATION

Am I learning to trust God's sovereignty in the everyday joy-robbers as well as my big problems? The zit that appears before a first date? The car that breaks down 10 miles from home and it's snowing? The phone that fails to ring when I want it to?

D. VERSE TO MEMORIZE THIS WEEK

Ps. 40:1–3a: "I waited patiently for the LORD; he turned to me and heard my cry. He lifted me out of the slimy pit, out of the mud and mire; he set my feet on a rock and gave me a firm place to stand."

E. THOUGHT TO CARRY HOME

Hannah took her pain to the right place, the right God, and she did the right thing. She poured out her heart to Him, and He gave her a song.

F. CREATIVE EXPRESSION

Take one or two key thoughts or verses from either Mary's or Hannah's song and personalize them, composing your own praise song. Write your song with *joy*._____

_____

_____

_____

_____

G. SELF-EVALUATION

1. What does my heart long for?
2. What causes me pain?
3. Have I poured out my needs and pain before God like Hannah did?
4. Am I expecting my God to fight for me and give me victory?
5. Considering all the things God has given me, am I holding them with an open hand, or am I shouting, "No! no!" and clenching them close to myself?
6. What step have I taken today to understand my God and His sovereignty?
7. In what ways can I express in actions my joy over who He is?

LESSON 21

DAVID, A MAN WHO SAW HIMSELF THROUGH GOD'S EYES

A. INTRODUCTION

Who are you? What are you like? How would you describe yourself to someone who has never met you? What key words would you use?_____

B. THINKING IT THROUGH

1. Through my *eyes*:

   a. Evaluation.

   Evaluate your self-description above. Does it contain descriptions of things you like to do (sports, music, drama, etc.)? Or are the descriptions *you* (height, hair color, personality, etc.)?

   1) Is it sometimes easier to tell someone what we *do* rather than to say who we *are*?_____

   2) Why is it hard to tell someone what we're really like?_____

   b. Information.

   Many circumstances have influenced us and shaped us into the people we are today. These influences cause us to think about ourselves the way we do.

   1) What influences/circumstances have shaped your life?

   _____   _____   _____

   _____   _____   _____

   _____   _____   _____

   _____   _____   _____

   _____   _____   _____

   2) What do you think the term *self-perception* means?_____

   3) In our early years we're fed a tremendous amount of data—some negative, some positive. We heard comments on how cute/ugly, fast/slow, agile/clumsy we were. How do you think this data affects our self-perception?_____

   4) Other data is comparative. "You're like your sister, except she never . . ." Give a comparison incident, either positive or negative, from your own life._____

   How did it make you feel?_____

   c. Reevaluation.

   We need to move our focus from the world's system of comparisons to God's eternal, unchanging evaluation of who we are.

1) What is comforting about God's evaluation of you? (Psa. 139:1–6)_____
_____
_____

2. Through God's eyes:
   a. To avoid frustration we must evaluate ourselves in the light of God's standard.
      1) What is the difference between God's evaluation of ourselves and the world's evaluation?_____
      _____
      2) Which is less frustrating?_____
         Why?_____
   b. Information.
      We need to reprogram our information. We've seen that our self-perception is largely formed on the information of others and the comparison of ourselves to others.
      A proper self-perception is based on the information given by our designer and creator—God.
      1) Read Ps. 139:13–16. How much does God know about you?_____
      _____
      2) Who is ultimately responsible for your existence? (139:13)_____
      3) What adjectives are used to describe you? (139:14)_____
      _____
      4) What does God know about your stature and physical limitations? (139:15)_____
      _____
      5) When God ordained your days, this involved not only _____ , but also _____ .
         (139:16)

C. CONTEMPORARY APPLICATION

1. Reevaluation time, ask yourself the following questions:
   a. What do I do with this new information? How can it help me think more clearly about who I am in God's eyes? in the world's eyes?
   b. Contrast parts of your old information with the new information you have gained from this lesson:

   Old information   New information

   _____   _____
   _____   _____
   _____   _____
   _____   _____

D. VERSE TO MEMORIZE THIS WEEK

Eph. 2:10: "For we are God's workmanship, created in Christ Jesus to do good works, which God prepared in advance for us to do."

E. THOUGHT TO CARRY HOME

I am specially designed by God, and I am of infinite worth to Him.

F. CREATIVE EXPRESSION

Have a hat party. Look at the various hats David wore—shepherd, harpist, fugitive, king.

What kind do you wear? brother? sister? son? daughter? basketball player? gymnast? musician? List your different hats. Underneath your list, write, "What I *do* flows from who I *am*, not the other way around."

_____
_____
_____
_____
_____

G. SELF-EVALUATION

1. Do I usually think of myself in terms of who I am or what I do?
2. What remarks made about me when I was younger do I still think are true?

3. How do I compare myself to others to see how I measure up?

4. Do I still want to be in this kind of comparison trap? What am I doing that feeds this comparison? What deprogramming do I need most?

5. What truth do I see from Psalm 139 that changes how I see myself?

6. What can I do to make my "new information" from God's Word part of my life?

LESSON 22

MEPHIBOSHETH, A HANDICAPPED MAN IN THE KING'S PALACE

A. INTRODUCTION
Define the terms *handicapped* and *disabled*._____
_____
_____

B. THINKING IT THROUGH
1. Preparation of a family (1 Sam. 20)
   a. What relationship does God prearrange to benefit Mephibosheth? (20:42)_____
   _____

   b. 1 Sam. 20:14–17 says that Jonathan made a covenant with the house of David. A covenant is a binding agreement between friends, a total commitment of oneself to another.
      1) Who was the witness to Jonathan and David's oath to each other? (20:23)_____

2. Accident (2 Sam. 4:4)
   a. How did Mephibosheth become crippled?_____

   b. How do you think Mephibosheth felt about himself as he was growing up?_____
   _____

   c. Do you think he ever wondered why God allowed the crippling accident? Why or why not?_____

3. Fulfillment of a promise (2 Sam. 9:1–13)
   a. Why did David want to be kind to Mephibosheth?_____

   b. What did David do?_____
   _____

   c. How did this make Mephibosheth feel?_____

   d. David recognized that not only did Mephibosheth need him, but David's sons needed Mephibosheth, too. How do you think Mephibosheth might have contributed to their lives?_____
   _____

   e. How can those who are different from us be part of our everyday lives?_____
   _____

   f. What can we expect to learn from them?_____
   They from us?_____

4. Is David more important than Mephibosheth in God's eyes? (1 Cor. 12:12–27). Why or why not?_____
   _____

5. Every year babies are born with handicaps, and children and young people become disabled through illness

or accident. What if it happened to you, to someone in your family, or to a friend? How would you handle it?_____

The following verses have ministered to many disabled persons. Look up these verses and write the key thought or phrase you feel to be most helpful.

    a. Deut. 33:25_____

    b. Ps. 33:22_____

    c. Ps. 91:4_____

    d. Isa. 41:10_____

    e. Heb. 2:18_____

    f. Heb. 4:14–15_____

    g. John 14:16–18_____

6. Paul said he had a "thorn in the flesh" that bothered him. Although scholars disagree on what the "thorn" might have been, it possibly was a physical disability of some kind. We know that Paul asked God three times for its removal (2 Cor. 12:7–10).

    a. In v. 9 God said, "_____

    _____"

    b. Weaknesses and disabilities, even diseases, are permitted in our lives to:

        1) v. 7_____

        2) v. 9_____

C. CONTEMPORARY APPLICATION

Do you see discrimination against handicapped and disabled people? Where? How does this fit in with the way God sees them? In His eyes we are all of equal worth. How will this truth affect the way you relate to those who are different?

D. VERSE TO MEMORIZE THIS WEEK

2 Cor. 12:9: "But he said to me, 'My grace is sufficient for you, for my power is made perfect in weakness.' Therefore I will boast all the more gladly about my weaknesses, so that Christ's power may rest on me."

E. THOUGHT TO CARRY HOME

People who have handicaps are every bit as valuable as those with no apparent disability. We are all equally valuable in God's eyes; we all have a contribution to make, no matter who we are.

F. CREATIVE EXPRESSION

Ask God for direction, then brainstorm ideas for the following situations:

    If you are like Mephibosheth or Paul, write down every idea that comes into your head about how you, an indispensable part of the body of Christ, might contribute to families like David's.

    If you are like David and his sons, write down every idea about how you might contribute to the lives of the Mephibosheths and Pauls of your world._____

_____

_____

    Jesus prayed that we all might be united in one spirit (John 17:20–23). Write a prayer asking God to make this happen in your relationships with others._____

_____

_____

G. SELF-EVALUATION

1. What changes would take place in my life if I became disabled this year?
2. Would I be bitter toward God if something like that happened?
3. What did I discover in today's lesson that would help me work through my feelings?
4. What is one thing I can do to make life better for a handicapped or disabled person I know?

LESSON 23

DANIEL, AN ORPHAN WHO NEEDED A FATHER

A. INTRODUCTION

What is an orphan? How does an orphan differ from a child from a broken home?_____
_____
_____

Deuteronomy 10:17–18 expresses God's special concern for the orphan. Fill in the blanks. "For the LORD your God is God of gods and Lord of lords, the great God, mighty and awesome, who shows no _____ and accepts no _____. He defends the cause of the _____ and the _____, and loves the _____, giving him _____ and _____."

B. THINKING IT THROUGH

Daniel was taken to Babylon, apparently because he was of the nobility, and he was young, strong and intelligent.

1. The capture of Daniel (2 Kings 24:3; Dan. 1:1–7)
   a. Why was Judah captured by the Babylonians? (2 Kings 24:3)._____
   _____
   _____

   b. Did God know this was going to happen? Compare 2 Kings 24:3 with Dan. 1:2. Why or why not?_____
   _____
   _____

   c. Why was Daniel taken? (Dan. 1:3–4)._____
      1) What qualifications was the king looking for in the young male captives?_____
      _____
      _____

      2) What was King Nebuchadnezzar's plan for the captured men?_____
      _____

2. The challenge faced by Daniel (Dan. 1:8–21)
   a. What orders are given to the chief official? (Dan. 1:5, 10)_____
   _____

   b. What is Daniel's response to them? (Dan. 1:8)_____
   _____

   c. Why does Daniel resist this VIP treatment? (Ex. 34:14–17)_____
   _____

   d. Who put sympathy and understanding into the official's heart? (Dan. 1:9)_____
   e. What fear does the official in charge of the program express to Daniel? (Dan. 1:10)_____
   _____
   _____

3. The commitment of Daniel (Dan. 1:15–20; 6:1–13)
   a. What was the result of the ten-day trial period? (Dan. 1:15–16)_____
   _____
   _____

   b. How does God bless Daniel's commitment? (Dan. 1:17–21)_____
   _____
   _____

4. The child/Father relationship between Daniel and God (Dan. 6:10–11)
   Daniel expressed his commitment to God and his dependence upon Him by praying. Jesus' dependent relationship with His heavenly Father was also expressed in prayer. See Mark 1:35; 6:45–47; Luke 5:15–16; 6:12–13; John 14:6–31.

1) Compare Jesus' relationship with His Father to Daniel's relationship to his God.

2) In John 14:6–31, how often does Jesus say "Father"? _____ In the verses listed above, how often do you see Jesus praying? _____ In Daniel 6:10b, 11, how often do you see Daniel praying? _____

C. CONTEMPORARY APPLICATION

Four areas explored in the child/Father relationship in Lesson 5 are: God as provider, protector, teacher, and nurturer. Examine the following verses and see how Daniel, the orphan, experiences God's fatherly touches on his life. Apply the truth you learn to your own life.

1. What physical needs does God provide for Daniel? (Dan. 1:15)_____

_____

For me?_____

2. How does God reveal himself as teacher to Daniel? (Dan. 1:17; 2:23)_____

_____

To me?_____

3. How does God protect Daniel? (Dan. 6:20–23)_____

_____

Me?_____

4. What does God express in His counsel to Daniel? (Dan. 10:19) (Clue: "highly esteemed" is translated "greatly beloved" in the KJV.)_____

_____

In His counsel to me?_____

D. VERSES TO MEMORIZE THIS WEEK

John 14:18 and Dan. 6:16b: "I will not leave you orphans; I will come to you." "May your God, whom you serve continually, rescue you!"

E. THOUGHT TO CARRY HOME

Daniel could have felt abandoned by God in a strange country, among ungodly people. Instead, he abandoned himself to God, his Father.

F. CREATIVE EXPRESSION

Explore the Father/child relationship further by asking yourself how you would feel if you received news that a special friend had just become an orphan. What would you tell your friend? How would you encourage him or her?

Write a letter expressing not only your love but your concern that your friend understand that God is a Father to the fatherless. Cite principles from Daniel's story or from Jesus' life to explain the close Father/child relationship God's children can count on. Include a verse that you feel best expresses what you want your friend to understand.

Dear_____ ,

_____
_____
_____
_____
_____
_____
_____

G. SELF-EVALUATION

1. Do I believe that God is in control of my life?
2. Do I believe that God, a loving God, could make or has made me an orphan?
3. How do I express my dependence in God, my Father?
4. Do I, like Daniel, pray often, or do I try to solve my problems on my own?
5. If my parents weren't around, would my belief in God be strong enough to survive ungodly influences?
6. How can I develop survival strength to stand up alone for what's right?
7. What am I doing now to develop that strength?

LESSON 24

ZECHARIAH, A MAN WHO DISCOVERED GOD'S GREATNESS

A. INTRODUCTION

Zechariah, a priest, is the first in our study of New Testament characters modeling our potential.

Read in Exodus 28 the instructions God gave Moses concerning the priest's clothing. Draw a sketch or write a description of them below. You may want to do both.

_____

_____

_____

_____

_____

_____

B. THINKING IT THROUGH (Luke 1:5–25, 39–80)

1. Write Luke's description of what Zechariah and his wife were like on the inside. (Luke 1:6)_____

_____

2. What was Zechariah doing in the temple?_____

3. What was happening outside the temple while Zechariah was inside?_____

4. What words describe Zechariah's reaction when the angel appears to him?_____

5. What does the angel say that reveals Zechariah as a man of prayer?_____

6. How does the angel describe the ministry of the child that Zechariah and Elizabeth will be given?

    a. _____   e. _____

    b. _____   f. _____

    c. _____   g. _____

    d. _____

7. What does the angel say that shows he detected doubt and unbelief in Zechariah's response?_____

_____

8. What happens to Zechariah as a result of that unbelief?_____

_____

9. During the events and conversations of Luke 1:39–56, Zechariah was a silent observer. Write your observations from his viewpoint in the words you think Zechariah might have used had he written it down in his journal that night._____

_____

_____

_____

10. When Mary returned to her family and her betrothed three months later, she went with Zechariah's silent commendation. He believed her story of a miraculous conception. As a priest, he knew the law. A woman could be stoned for committing adultery. Why do you think he didn't condemn her?_____

_____

11. Zechariah's silent days continued. We can know he grew in his knowledge of God during these silent months by the song he sang when God opened his lips. Which phrase in Zechariah's song (Luke 1:68–79) clearly indicates Zechariah spent time in the Scriptures, listening to God?_____

_____

12. Examine Zechariah's song and compare with Mary's and Hannah's songs studied in Lesson 21.

    a. Complete the following sentences that show the similarities and differences between them. Compare the first line of each song. Note that all three songs are pure praise songs. They ask for nothing; they simply exult in who God is.

        1) The attribute of God that all three singers mention is _____ . Hannah mentions it _____ time; Mary, _____ time; Zechariah mentions it or a form of it _____ times.

        2) All three talk of God's _____ as seen in compassion for the sorrowing and helpless.

        3) All three sing of God's power and strength. Mary sings about Him performing _____ ____ with His arm; Hannah mentions His _____ from heaven against the wicked; Zechariah refers to his coming and _____ His people.

        5) Hannah calls God her _____ ; Mary rejoices in _____ ; Zechariah exalts Him as the_____ _____ .

        6) Both Zechariah and Hannah sing about the _____ (strength) lifted high.

        7) Zechariah reveals a heart sensitive to beauty in 1:78–79 when he talks about the rising sun.

    b. Put these verses in your own words._____

_____

_____

_____

    c. Turn your creative talents to art. Sketch how you see these same verses.

C. CONTEMPORARY APPLICATION

While you're in a group setting sometime this week, try to concentrate the entire time on listening instead of talking. What do you observe?

While you're alone, turn off the TV, stereo, or whatever you usually listen to and tune in to God for a half hour. Turn to Luke 1 and pick out the attributes of God that Zechariah sang about. Be still and know that He is God.

D. VERSE TO MEMORIZE THIS WEEK

Ps. 46:10: "Be still, and know that I am God; I will be exalted among the nations, I will be exalted in the earth."

E. THOUGHT TO CARRY HOME

Shutting my mouth and opening my ears to listen to others and to God can deepen my relationships and teach me more about who my God is.

F. CREATIVE EXPRESSION

Practice listening by turning off your mouth and opening the ears of your soul while you complete this sentence: "Listening to God is . . ." Add words, verses, phrases, pictures, etc.

G. SELF-EVALUATION

1. What have I learned about listening to God from Zechariah's life?
2. What impresses me about his attentiveness?
3. What do I allow to intrude into my listening times in Sunday school? worship hour? my private prayer time?
4. Have I ever simply praised God for who He is without asking for something?
5. What attribute or character quality of God did Zechariah recognize that I need to learn more about?
6. What can I do this week to make that become a reality in my life?

LESSON 25

JOHN THE BAPTIST, A MAN WHO DARED TO BE DIFFERENT

A. INTRODUCTION

A "gimper" is a person who aspires to excel, to be different.

John the Baptist could be called a gimper. Look for these qualities as you work your way through the following questions.

B. THINKING IT THROUGH

1. John the Baptist's ministry was prophesied by both Isaiah and Malachi. (Isa. 40:3; Mal. 3:1)
   a. Isaiah said he would be a_____
   b. Malachi said he would be a_____
2. Write down the phrase that describes how John grew on the inside. (Luke 1:80)_____

3. We next see him as a fiery man of God calling people to repentance.
   a. Describe his physical appearance. (Matt. 3:4)_____
   _____
   _____

   b. Describe his ministry. (John 1:6–7)_____
   _____
   _____

4. Develop a character portrait of John the Baptist by studying these scripture portions.

a. John the Baptist's purpose (Luke 3:1–18)

   1) How did John view the coming Messiah? (Luke 3:16)_____

   _____

   2) What kind of word picture does he use to describe Him? (vv. 17–18)_____

   _____

   3) How does John view himself? (vv. 4–6, 16)_____

   _____

   _____

   4) How does the crowd respond to John? (vv. 10, 12, 14)_____

   _____

   5) How does John respond to the crowd (v. 11)_____

   _____

   to the tax collectors?_____

   to the soldiers?_____

   Application question: What do you think John would say to you if you asked the same questions these people asked?_____

   _____

b. John the Baptist's testimony (John 1:6–37)

   1) A testimony is a public declaration or statement to establish a fact. Summarize what John testifies about Jesus Christ. (John 1:6–18, 29, 34)_____

   _____

   _____

   _____

   2) Who does John say he himself is? (John 1:20–23)_____

   _____

   3) Write your own testimony of who you believe Jesus to be._____

   _____

   _____

c. John the Baptist's relationship with Jesus (John 3:27–36; Matt. 3:13–17)

   1) How does John see his relationship with Jesus? (John 3:28–30)_____

   _____

   _____

   2) What unique privilege did John receive? (Matt. 3:13–17)_____

   _____

   3) How did John feel about it?_____

   _____

   4) Write down specific truths that John believes about Jesus. (John 3:31–35)_____

   _____

   Application question: How would you describe your relationship with Jesus?_____

   _____

d. John the Baptist's imprisonment (Matt. 11:1–14; Matt. 14:1–12)

   1) How does Jesus respond to John's disciples? (Matt. 11:4–6)_____

   _____

   2) What does he tell the crowd about John? (Matt. 11:7–9)_____

   _____

   3) What do Jesus' words reveal about His feelings for John? (Matt. 11:11–14)_____

   _____

   4) How does Herod feel about John? (Matt. 14:3–5)_____

   _____

5) What was the response of John's disciples after they buried John? (Matt. 14:12)_____

    Application questions: How do I respond when I hurt?_____

_____

    Do I ever tell Jesus about it? Ps. 62:8 invites me to_____

_____

5. Write a descriptive paragraph about John the Baptist, summarizing the gimper qualities you've discovered about him._____

_____

_____

_____

6. Jesus taught gimper living. What did He tell the people to do that is descriptive of that kind of lifestyle? Matt. 5:41, 44; 10:42_____

_____

7. List the action that expresses a "gimper" quality of life in the following verses:

    2 Cor. 8:7_____

    1 Thess. 4:1_____

    1 Thess. 4:10_____

    1 Cor. 15:58_____

C. CONTEMPORARY APPLICATION

Being out of step with society isn't the "in" thing. Yet those who have made significant contributions were people who dared to think creatively, move out of the norm, and act boldly. Jesus wants you to be a "gimper."

D. VERSE TO MEMORIZE THIS WEEK

Matthew 10:39: "Whoever finds his life will lose it, and whoever loses his life for my sake will find it."

E. THOUGHT TO CARRY HOME

John the Baptist lived his brief life to the hilt. He attacked it with everything he had. He did it enthusiastically, courageously, and humbly.

F. CREATIVE EXPRESSION

A metaphor is a word picture in which one thing is likened to another. Metaphors help us clarify our understanding of ourselves.

    John referred to himself in the metaphor of a voice crying in the wilderness.

    Write your own metaphor of how you feel about yourself or your purpose in life. I am_____

      OR

    Write a metaphor that describes your relationship with Jesus. (Jesus used metaphors to describe himself and us: I am the vine, you are the branches; I am the shepherd, you are the sheep.)_____

_____

G. SELF-EVALUATION

1. Which "gimper" quality of John the Baptist's is most lacking in my life?
2. Which quality in his life do I most admire?
3. Which "gimper" quality of life that Jesus describes do I most desire?
4. What choices do I need to make in order for these qualities to become evident in my life? What step of obedience is God asking me to take today?

LESSON 26

MARY OF BETHANY, A WOMAN WHO WORSHIPED

A. INTRODUCTION

Define worship._____

_____

_____

    Mary of Bethany was a woman whose understanding of Jesus surpassed that of the men. Mary had grasped the meaning of His mission to earth. She knew He faced the cross. Jesus acknowledged this when she poured nard (an expensive perfume) on His head and feet in an act of adoration and worship before His death.

B. THINKING IT THROUGH

1. Our first glimpse of Mary (Luke 10:38–42)
   a. Describe the picture you see as you read these verses._____

   _____

   _____

   b. What positive personality traits do you see in the sisters?
   1) Martha (v. 38)_____
   2) Mary (v. 39)_____
2. The sisters see Jesus' resurrection power (John 11:1–44)
   a. What kind of relationship do you sense this family has with Jesus by the message the sisters send to Jesus? (vv. 3, 5)_____

   _____

   b. How does Jesus respond to their message? (vv. 5–6)_____

   _____

   c. How long had Lazarus been in the tomb by the time Jesus arrived? (v. 17)_____
   d. What does Martha do when she hears He's coming from Jerusalem to Bethany? (v. 20)_____
   1) What does she say to Him?_____

   _____

   2) By what title does Jesus express His power? (v. 25)_____

   _____

   3) Who does Martha say she believes Jesus to be? (v. 27)_____

   _____

   e. How do you think Mary feels as she sits waiting for Jesus?_____

   _____

   1) Have you ever felt hurt or had deep needs, yet Jesus seemed far away or didn't seem to respond? Enter into Mary's hurt by writing an entry she might have written in her journal while she waited.____

   _____

   _____

   _____

   _____

   f. What was Mary's response when Martha told her Jesus was asking for her? (vv. 28–33)_____

   _____

   g. What was Jesus' response to Mary's tears? (vv. 33–35)_____

   _____

   h. Write a journal entry Mary might have written after Jesus raised her brother Lazarus from the dead. Express her wonder and joy. (vv. 38–44)_____

   _____

_____

_____

3. Mary worships at Jesus' feet (Matt. 26:6–13; Mark 14:3–9; John 12:1–9)
   a. Write down your observations from the three accounts.
   Matt. 26:6–13_____

_____

_____

   Mark 14:3–9_____

_____

_____

_____

   John 12:1–9_____

_____

_____

To worship means to respond to God. Mary responded to Jesus' love by doing what she could, giving what she had. Jesus said (Mark 14:8), "_____
_____."

Mary's sacrifice was symbolized in the pouring out of her most valued possession. Her life and love is symbolized by the fragrance poured out on her Lord. Mary gave all. She worshiped at His feet.

C. CONTEMPORARY APPLICATION
1. How would you explain worship to someone who missed this lesson?_____

_____

   a. If God shows me sin in my life, I respond by_____
   b. When He shows me His sacrifice on the cross, I respond by_____
   c. When he shows me the power of His resurrection, I respond by_____

D. VERSE TO MEMORIZE THIS WEEK
Rom. 12:1: "Therefore, I urge you, brothers, in view of God's mercy, to offer your bodies as living sacrifices, holy and pleasing to God—which is your spiritual worship."

E. THOUGHT TO CARRY HOME
Mary of Bethany believed that Jesus was worthy of her worship. Her act is a memorial of love poured out on her Lord.

F. CREATIVE EXPRESSION
Jesus prophesied that wherever Mary's name would be mentioned, her act of devotion would be spoken of as a memorial to her. Describe Mary's act of worship by creating an acrostic. Follow the pattern given, and next to Mary's, do one with your own name.

M
A
R
Y

O
F

B
E
T
H
A
N
Y

G. SELF-EVALUATION

1. How are you making worship an everyday part of your life?
2. How are you applying the Word to your own life so that it can be a fragrance to others?
3. Look back to when you first began this study on building a proper self-concept. Is there an area where you see growth in knowing who God is? who you are?
4. How has that understanding changed you?

LESSON 27

BARNABAS, THE VIP OF ENCOURAGEMENT

A. INTRODUCTION

1. Who wrote the Book of Acts?_____
2. What character quality does Luke depict in both Jesus and Barnabas?_____
_____
3. Define encouragement._____
_____

Barnabas, the Levite from Cyprus appears and reappears in the Book of Acts. Luke, the writer of Acts, is the one who shows us Barnabas, the comforter.

Luke's gospel shows the ministry of compassion Jesus had to the hurting, sick, and brokenhearted. Both Luke and Barnabas knew Jesus, the God of compassion. (Read Luke 4:18; 5:12, 13; 7:46–50; 13:11–13; 13:34; 18:15–16.)

B. THINKING IT THROUGH

1. Barnabas, models for us the ministry of encouragement. We first meet him in Acts 4:32–37.
   a. What was the meaning of the name the apostles gave him?_____
   b. What kind of encouragement do we see him giving to this persecuted, struggling church body?_____
2. How do we see Barnabas ministering to Saul? (Acts 9:18–31). (Read the entire chapter if you're unfamiliar with Saul's background.)_____
_____

   a. What was the reaction of the disciples in Jerusalem to Saul?_____
_____

   b. What two things does Barnabas do?_____
_____

   c. What were the results of Barnabas's personal ministry to Saul?_____
_____

3. How do we see Barnabas ministering to the new church body in Antioch? (Acts 11:19–30)_____
_____

   a. What was happening at the Antioch church?_____
_____

   b. What was the response of the church in Jerusalem when they heard the news?_____
_____

   c. What do you think Barnabas might have said to encourage them to remain true to the Lord with all their hearts?_____
_____

d. What would you say to someone who was struggling to remain true to the Lord?_____
_____

What verse would you share?_____
e. Acts 11:24 describes Barnabas and his ministry. Would you say he was successful?_____
f. What insight do you gain from his going to Tarsus to bring back Saul to help?_____
_____

1) Into what position does Barnabas push Saul?_____
2) What is the significance of the shift in name placement? (Acts 13:2, 42)_____
_____

3) Would it be hard for you to encourage another to take your place in a position where you had been successful?_____

4) How did Barnabas's ministry reflect Paul's teaching in Phil. 2:1–4?_____

4. How does Barnabas prove himself as an encourager to John Mark? (Acts 15:36–41)_____
_____

a. How would you describe John Mark's record at that point? (Acts 13:13)_____
_____

b. What was the result of Barnabas's wanting to give John Mark another chance?_____
_____

c. Imagine the discussion between Barnabas and Saul.
Paul: "No. There's too much at stake. He failed once. We can't risk it a second time."
Barnabas: "You're wrong. He's showing spiritual growth, and needs to know he has a ministry. He'll succeed if we encourage . . .
(You finish the dialogue.)_____
_____
_____
_____
_____

5. Summarize Barnabas's ministry. In what four ways did Barnabas prove himself an encouragement?
through_____
through_____
through_____
through_____
Barnabas's ministry could be summed up in one sentence: He made beautiful background music for others.

C. CONTEMPORARY APPLICATION

Think about last week. Were you more of an encourager or discourager? What can you do this week to encourage someone else? Actively look for someone who needs a boost up.

D. VERSES TO MEMORIZE THIS WEEK

Galatians 6:9–10: "Let us not become weary in doing good, for at the proper time we will reap a harvest if we do not give up. Therefore, as we have opportunity, let us do good to all people, especially to those who belong to the family of believers."

E. THOUGHT TO CARRY HOME

Seeing our God as a God of compassion, comfort, and encouragement enables us to become as Barnabas was, a minister of encouragement to others.

F. CREATIVE EXPRESSION

Do you know anyone who makes beautiful background music for another? Write a short description of a "Barnabas" you've observed. This person might be within your circle of friends or an older or younger person in your

church. Tell specifically what action this person took that encouraged you or someone else._____
_____
_____

G. SELF-EVALUATION

1. Have I been able to participate in the life of an individual or a church through giving? through coming alongside another? through giving preference to another? through giving a failure a boost up? How?
2. Which area of encouragement modeled by Barnabas challenged me most? Why?

LESSON 28

PAUL, A MAN WHO UNDERSTOOD SERVANTHOOD

A. INTRODUCTION

Called to be the Apostle to the Gentiles, used by God as prolific epistle writer, Paul still considered himself a mere bondservant for Jesus Christ.

1. Before he preached about Jesus, Paul describes his actions toward the early church (Acts 22:4; 26:10–11) as
_____
_____
_____
_____
_____

B. THINKING IT THROUGH

1. The first words that come from Saul's lips after Jesus stops him on the Damascus road are (Acts 22:8)_____
_____

2. His next question is (Acts 22:10)_____
   a. How does Paul address Jesus?_____
   b. What do you remember about that name from Lesson 6?_____
   _____

3. Paul responded to His Lord (*Adonai*) by going away to be alone with his Lord for preparation to be a bondservant. How does he describe his actions in Gal. 1:15–17?_____
   _____

4. A bondservant is one who willingly places himself under the authority of another (Ex. 21:2–6). How can we know that this is Paul's attitude? (1 Cor. 3:5)_____
   _____

   a. Paul sees himself as a _____ . He sees Jesus as _____ .
   b. What application can you make to your own life from his words?_____
   _____

5. What is Paul's life goal? (Phil. 3:8, 10)_____
   _____
   _____
   _____
   _____

6. Knowing Jesus intimately enabled Paul to be a true bondservant to God and to others. When he looked at Jesus Christ, he saw the perfect servant modeled.
   a. Isa. 42:1–7 sketches a word picture of how God sees His Son, His servant in whom He delights. Choose

64

a verse from this section and paraphrase it into your own expression of joy in the servanthood of Jesus Christ._____

_____

b. Write down your observations about servanthood from the following verses:
Exodus 21:2–6 *with* Ps. 40:6–8 and Heb. 10:7; Phil. 2:7–8_____

_____

John 8:29; Rom. 15:3_____

_____

Matt. 20:28; Luke 22:27_____

How did Jesus set an example of servanthood? (John 13:13–16)_____

_____

c. What is the alternative to being Jesus' servant? (Rom. 6:16)_____

_____

d. Contrast the service to which Jesus calls us, with the service the world demands. (1 Cor. 7:22; Rom. 6:22)

_____

_____

8. Discover the practical aspect of servanthood by examining the following verses: Phil. 2:3–4; Phil. 4:8; Heb. 10:24; Rom. 12:15 *with* Heb. 13:3. Either list the servant attitudes you discover, or personalize a servant attitude, using one or more of these verses._____

_____

_____

_____

C. CONTEMPORARY APPLICATION

The world shouts, "Look out for yourself! Push yourself forward. Be aggressive and you'll get what you want."

But the Word teaches there is exaltation in servanthood not only later but now. Discover for yourself a servant's joy by doing the specific servant suggestion under this lesson's Creative Expression.

D. VERSES TO MEMORIZE THIS WEEK

Matt. 20:26–28: "Instead, whoever wants to become great among you must be your servant, and whoever wants to be first must be your slave just as the Son of Man did not come to be served, but to serve, and to give his life as a ransom for many."

E. THOUGHT TO CARRY HOME

Servanthood is the result of my relationship with my Master. Servanthood is being available to meet another's need with simplicity and humility.

F. CREATIVE EXPRESSION

Write your personal response to Paul's appeal in Rom. 12:1–2. If you truly desire Jesus to be your Lord in the fullest sense of the word, address your prayer, "Lord, Master, or *Adonai*."_____

_____

_____

Ask Him what He would have you do. (Acts 22:10)_____

_____

Write down the person He impresses on your heart as you ask, "Whom do I know who's hurting today?"
_____ "How can I be a servant to that one today?" Be specific. (Thought-starters: Write a note, give them a smile, do something they need to have done, etc.)_____

_____

Later, record how you felt after you did your servant action._____

_____

G. SELF-EVALUATION

1. Do I recognize God's right of ownership on my life?
2. Can I call myself God's bondservant?
3. Have I understood that He wants all of me—not just my time or talents—but me?
4. Do I recognize that God has my highest good in mind when He says (through Paul), "I urge you . . . in view of God's mercy, to offer your bodies as living sacrifices, holy and pleasing to God—which is your spiritual worship."
5. Do I recognize that servanthood is an attitude of self-giving?

LESSON 29

JOHN, A DISCIPLE WHO KNEW GOD INTIMATELY

A. INTRODUCTION

The disciple John was with Jesus from the beginning of His ministry. Some Bible scholars feel that John was the other disciple with Andrew who first followed Jesus.

1. What did Jesus invite these disciples to do when they asked Him where He was staying? (John 1:35–40)

2. While John and his brother James were fishing, Jesus called them to follow Him. How did they respond? (Mark 1:16–20)

3. John's relationship with his Master grew and deepened. How does John refer to himself in John 13:23?

4. When Jesus commits to John the care of His mother, what does that indicate about the relationship between Jesus and John? (John 19:25–27)

B. THINKING IT THROUGH

1. John's ministry after Jesus' ascension into heaven:
   a. What five books of the Bible did John write through the inspiration of the Spirit? _____, _____, _____, _____, _____

   b. John received the special privilege of recording the unveiling of Jesus Christ in the last book of the Bible (Rev. 1). Consult an atlas or Bible dictionary and write down what you discover about the tiny island of Patmos.

   c. The Book John is told to write is not intended to conceal truth but to reveal Jesus Christ. What is the promise to those who read its message and take it to heart? (Rev. 1:3)

   d. How does John describe himself in Revelation 1:1, 9?

   e. Put your powers of observation to work to dig out details from Rev. 1:9–12. Answer the following questions:
      1) Where is John?
      2) Why is he there?
      3) What day is it?
      4) What does the voice speaking to John sound like?
      5) Where does it come from?
      6) What is he asked to do?

7) What is John's response?_____

8) What does he see?_____

f. Write John's description of Jesus by filling in the blanks (Rev. 1:12–16). He was dressed in _____.
His head and hair were like _____.His eyes were like _____.His feet were like
_____.His voice like _____.His right hand held _____.A_____
came from His mouth. His face was like _____ .

1) What color predominates this description?_____

g. John is permitted to see Jesus in His majestic glory.

1) What is John's response?_____

2) How does Christ reassure him?_____

3) What words does Jesus use to describe who He is? (Rev. 1:18)_____
_____

4) What command does He reaffirm to John? (Rev. 1:19)_____
_____

h. Jesus is further revealed in Revelation 21. Read Revelation 21:3–4 and write down the phrases that reveal
Him as a personal God._____
_____

i. There are three classes of people described in Rev. 21:6–8: those who (v. 6) _____ , those who
(v. 7)_____ , and those who (v. 8)_____.

j. Each disciple is asked to join in Jesus' final invitation to all people (Rev. 22:17). Write it here._____
_____
_____

k. What was His promise? (Rev. 22:20)_____

2. Summarize your impression from today's lesson of who Jesus is. Include details from John and Jesus' relationship on earth and John's vision of Jesus, the glorious, powerful, risen Christ._____
_____
_____
_____
_____

C. CONTEMPORARY APPLICATION

Which group are you in?

1. Those who have accepted the gift of salvation, then gone on as though nothing significant has happened.
2. Those who have accepted, then given their entire selves as Jesus' disciples, those who are willing to follow
   Him anywhere, no matter what.
3. Those who stand outside the city, separated from God, destined for hell.

   Put a star beside the one where you fit. Put a ? beside the one where you think your best friend is. Put an
   * beside the one you want you and your friend to be in.

D. VERSE TO MEMORIZE THIS WEEK

Revelation 21:7: "He who overcomes will inherit all this, and I will be his God and he will be my son."

E. THOUGHT TO CARRY HOME

A disciple is an overcomer who shares a place of special intimacy with his God, both here on earth and in the
future city of God.

F. CREATIVE EXPRESSION

The dictionary says that to overcome means to be victorious; win. A banner denotes victory. "We will shout for
joy when you are victorious and will lift up our banners in the name of our God" (Ps. 20:5). Banners (the word
means easily seen) were erected on poles and hilltops to rally armies to victory.

Special promises are made to overcomers in Revelation 2 and 3. They can be transformed into illustrations of truth. Use these pictures liberally as you design an overcomers banner in the space below. (See Rev. 2:7; 10–11, 17, 26–28; 3:5, 12, 21.)

Share your banner with someone who may be weary and needing encouragement.

G. SELF-EVALUATION

1. Am I developing an intimate relationship with Jesus?
2. Am I spending prime time in His Word, learning who HE IS?
3. In what ways am I paying the high cost of discipleship?
4. What am I doing for my friend who's standing on the brink of hell?
5. If I were to take this lesson seriously, I would have to_____

_____

LESSON 30

CHOOSE YOUR OWN CHARACTER

This lesson is designed for you to express in your own words the impact of one character's life on your own. The following questions are given to help you think through the person's life with whom you most identify.

How do you think _____ sees himself/herself?

How do you think _____ sees God?

How is God revealing himself to _____ ?

How is _____ concept of God affecting his/her behavior?

What strengths do I see in _____ life? what weaknesses?

What strengths does _____ show that can be a model for me?

What weakness does _____ reveal that I most identify with?

What can I learn from the way _____ handled his/her weakness that will help me deal with my own?

Ask your God, "What truth are you trying to teach me through this person's life? How can I let that truth change me into the person you most want me to become?"

A. CHARACTER AND TITLE

_____

_____

_____

_____

_____
_____
_____
_____
_____
_____
_____
_____
_____
_____
_____
_____
_____
_____
_____
_____
_____
_____

B. APPLICATION OF TRUTH TO MY LIFE

_____
_____
_____
_____
_____
_____
_____
_____

C. VERSE TO MEMORIZE THIS WEEK

Hebrews 12:1: "Therefore, since we are surrounded by such a great cloud of witnesses, let us throw off everything that hinders and the sin that so easily entangles, and let us run with perseverance the race marked out for us."

D. THOUGHT TO CARRY HOME

God has shared with us varied personalities within the pages of His Word. In each life he reveals Himself as the one true God, willing and able to meet any needs of the one who seeks Him.

E. CREATIVE EXPRESSION

Choose an object that reminds you of your character. Sketch it below. Write the verse that best expresses your character's life.

_____
_____
_____

Write the verse you've selected as your life verse._____

_____

Tell how you chose it and why._____

_____

_____

_____

SECTION IV

SEEING MY POSSIBILITIES: GOD AND I—WHAT A TEAM!

"All authority . . . has been given to me. Therefore go . . . and surely I will be with you always, to the very end of the age" (Matt. 28:18–20).

Section Objective: To understand that each person in the body of Christ is a vital part of God's team, impacting the world for Him.

LESSON 31

DEVELOPING A PRODUCTIVE LIFESTYLE

A. INTRODUCTION

Illustrate the parable of the Sower in Luke 8:5–8: a field, a simple figure of a farmer with an outstretched arm, seeds drifting from hand to ground. Add a path alongside, rocks tumbled beside it, soaring birds overhead and on the ground behind the sower.

B. THINKING IT THROUGH

Farming basics: plowing and planting, after that the harvest (Luke 8:5–15).

1. Understanding the parable (Luke 8:11–15)
   a. What is the seed?_____
   b. Who are the birds a picture of?_____
   c. Match each soil type with the "heart condition" it describes.

Luke 8:13—rocky soil	unbelieving heart (seed snatched away)
Luke 8:12—hard, compacted soil	saved but immature fruit
Luke 8:14—thorny soil	saved but no fruit
Luke 8:15—good soil	receptive, fruitful Christian

   (Note that it is always the same seed, but not always the same soil.)
   d. More about the seed from the Book of James:
      1) What does James say we should do with the seed planted in our hearts? (James 1:21)_____
      2) What is the purpose of God's Word within us? (1:18)_____

e. Look up the following scripture passages and explain how they illustrate the "seed verse" given.

1) Luke 8:12; John 12:20–37 _____

_____

_____

2) Luke 8:13; John 6:53–66 _____

_____

_____

3) Luke 8:14; Luke 18:18–25 _____

_____

_____

4) Luke 8:15; Luke 8:1–3 _____

_____

_____

f. Give an example of the four heart responses from people you know or have heard about.

1) Luke 8:12 _____

_____

_____

2) Luke 8:13 _____

_____

_____

3) Luke 8:14 _____

_____

_____

4) Luke 8:15 _____

_____

_____

g. Do a soil test on the following people's hearts, using a scale of 1–10 (10 is rock hard, 1 is soft).

1) Joanna (Luke 8:3) _____
2) John (Rev. 1:9) _____
3) Uzziah (2 Chron. 26:4–5, 16) _____
4) Demas (2 Tim. 4:10) _____
5) Elymus (Acts 13:6–10) _____

h. Summarize this parable of the Sower and Seeds by adding the labels from question 1c and sketches of the planting results to your drawing in the Introduction activity of this lesson: the seed on the hard pathway that never sprouts and is snatched away by birds; a withered sprout on hard, rocky ground with a burning sun directly overhead; thorns and an immature grain stalk side by side; a fully developed stalk of grain in the well-tilled field.

i. The lives of those whose soil is soft and productive are pictured in the verses below. Write a brief description of each.

1) Luke 8:16 _____
2) Ps. 1:1–3 _____

_____

3) Ps. 126:5–6 _____

_____

2. What, then, is our responsibility? How can we keep our hearts soft and receptive to the plantings of the Spirit of God? How can we produce a good harvest?

a. Pick out the phrase in John 15:5 that reflects our dependency on Jesus. _____

_____

b. This dependency is expressed through
  1) Eph. 6:18–20_____
  2) Col. 3:16_____
  3) John 15:1, 2; Heb. 12:11, perseverance in spite of_____
  4) James 1:2–4, 12_____
  5) Gal. 6:7–9_____
  6) diligence in personal growth (2 Pet. 1:5–8, list the qualities) _____ + _____ + _____ + _____ + _____ + _____ + _____ + _____ + _____ , which results in fruit-bearing.

  c. List the fruit in Gal. 5:22–23. _____ , _____ , _____ , _____ , _____ , _____ , _____ , _____ , _____ .

C. CONTEMPORARY APPLICATION

Do a soil test on your heart. Be honest. On a scale of one to ten, how do you rate? _____ .

Very soft   Rock hard
1   2   3   4   5   6   7   8   9   10

D. VERSES TO THINK ON THIS WEEK

James 1:16–18; 2 Pet. 1:3–8; Gal. 6:7–9

E. THOUGHT TO CARRY HOME

The fruit in my life is dependent on the Spirit within, where God's seed has been planted. But the condition of the soil in my heart is my responsibility.

F. CREATIVE EXPRESSION

Write a harvest song by paraphrasing parts of the following verses and arranging them in any order you would like: Ps. 126:5–6; 144:12–13; 145:15–16; 147:7, 14._____

_____

_____

_____

G. SELF-EVALUATION

1. What character quality has God shown me that He wants to develop in my life?
2. In what ways have I demonstrated fruitfulness this week?
3. How does the way I use my time reflect the importance or lack of importance God's Word has in my life?
4. How is the condition of my heart soil being expressed in my life?
5. What thorns might be choking out the good seed?
6. Has God used me to help till the soil and plant the seed in someone's life?

LESSON 32

HEARING AND DOING

A. INTRODUCTION

Draw a simple figure of a person with ears and a heart. Pencil a line from the ears, to the mind, to the heart, and on out through the hands and feet.

> "[Hear] is often used for listening to the Word of God with a firm purpose to obey His commands."
> —Cruden's Complete Concordance

1. How, then, should we "hear" God's Word?_____
_____

2. What has God planted in our hearts that makes this a reality in our lives? (James 1:21; Luke 8:15)_____
_____

B. THINKING IT THROUGH

1. Practicing what they preached was a problem for the Pharisees. (Matt. 23:1–4, 25)
   a. Has it ever been a problem for you? _____ How?_____
   _____

   b. What dishwashing instructions does Jesus give in 23:26?_____
   _____

   c. To what does He liken the cup?_____
   _____

   d. Has Jesus ever said those same words to you? _____ How do they make you feel? _____.
   What can you do about them?_____
   _____

2. You are there (Matt. 5:1–2; 7:24–27)
   a. Where?_____
   b. What story does Jesus use to summarize His sermon?_____
   _____

   c. What truth does it convey to you?_____
   _____

   d. When will you put it into actions?_____
   _____

   e. How will you do it?_____
   _____

3. Read Jesus' words in Matt. 7:24–27 and James 1:22–24. Write a comparison of the word pictures they use and the truth it illustrates. Notice how they both contrast the one who hears and acts with the one who doesn't.
   _____
   _____
   _____
   _____
   _____
   _____

4. Jesus and James both contrast the foolish with the wise in the verses above. James makes another contrast in 3:13–18.
   a. What is the opposite of evil practices? (v. 17)_____
   b. What is opposite of disorder? (17–18)_____
   c. List wisdom's characteristics in James 3:17–18:
      1) _____   5) _____
      2) _____   6) _____
      3) _____   7) _____
      4) _____   8) _____
   d. What special promise is given to peacemakers in 3:18?_____
   _____

   e. What promise does Jesus give to them in Matt. 5:9?_____
   _____

   Personalize: I can be a peacemaker this week by_____
   _____

5. James stresses that faith without deeds is dead (James 2:26). List the specific deeds James calls our attention to in the verses below.
   a. James 1:26–27_____

    b. 2:1–7 _____

    _____

    c. 2:8–13 _____

    _____

    d. 2:14–19 _____

    _____

    e. 2:20–26 _____

    _____

C. CONTEMPORARY APPLICATION

Consider this statement:

    "Sow a thought, reap an action.

    Sow an action, reap a habit,

    Sow a habit, reap a lifestyle,

    Sow a lifestyle, reap a destiny."

If your "sowing" continues as it is now, what will you be reaping?

D. VERSES TO THINK ON THIS WEEK

James 2:26; 3:13, 17–18; Matt. 7:24

E. THOUGHT TO CARRY HOME

A faith kept alive must be practiced. Build your house—your life—on God's Word, God's will, and God's work.

F. CREATIVE EXPRESSION

Choose one of the following questions:

1. Write a contemporary example of the wise man and the foolish man. How would their building turn out?

    _____

    _____

2. Finish this sentence. "If I am to take this lesson seriously, I must _____

    _____."

Summarization: My life must be built according to God's specifications.

G. SELF-EVALUATION

1. What has God planted inside my heart?
2. How is it expressed by my mouth? my actions?
3. On a scale of 1 to 10, how would I rate my "doing" last week?
4. What have I heard about today that I'm not "doing"?
5. If my "hearing" was the music and my "doing" the words, would they go together?

LESSON 33

FITTING INTO THE BODY OF CHRIST

A. INTRODUCTION

Define the church as described by Paul in Ephesians 1:22–23: Christ is the _____ , redeemed children of God are the _____ .

B. THINKING IT THROUGH

1. Write a description of the early church (Acts 2:42–47) _____

    _____

_____

_____

_____

Compare it with your own church. Note the similarities and differences._____

_____

_____

_____

2. The parts of the Body (1 Cor. 12:12–26)
   a. List the body parts Paul uses to describe the church:1) _____ , 2) _____ ,
      3) _____ ,4) _____ , 5) _____
   b. How has God arranged the parts in the body? (12:18)_____

      _____
   c. How does God view the body parts? (12:22)_____
   d. What does he say about the parts that seem to be weaker? (12:22–24)_____

      _____
   e. Why should we consider the body parts to be of equal importance? (12:25–26)_____

      _____

      Application question: Which body part do you think best describes you (your place in the body)?

      _____

      Why?_____

      _____

3. One of the problems we face is that we view the church as a place of meetings instead of as the body of Christ.
   Discover two reasons why meetings are important (Heb. 10:24–25).
   a. _____
   b. _____

4. Look up the following verses and discover opportunities for growth and service that the church gives us.
   a. Eph. 5:19–20_____
   b. 1 Tim. 4:13_____
   c. Matt. 18:20; Acts 12:12_____
   d. 1 Cor. 11:2_____
   e. 1 Cor. 16:2_____

5. God has given each believer a spiritual gift to enable her or him to serve the body. Compare the three lists
   Paul gives in his letters.

1 Cor. 12:28–31	Eph. 4:11–15	Rom. 12:6–8
_____	_____	_____
_____	_____	_____
_____	_____	_____
_____	_____	_____
_____	_____	_____
_____		_____

   One of the ways we discover our spiritual gifts is by taking advantage of opportunities to minister to others.
   Name one of the ways you ministered this past year._____
   What did you learn about yourself by doing it?_____

   _____

6. God blends your personality with your individual strengths and weaknesses, talents, environment, heritage,
   interests, and spiritual gifts into a person uniquely you. Ask yourself:
   a. What do I see about me that makes me uniquely me?_____

   _____

b. What talents do I have?_____

_____

c. How does my family differ from the neighbor's family?_____

_____

d. What do I see as my family's strengths?_____

_____

weaknesses?_____

e. How has God used me to minister to someone this week?_____

_____

C. CONTEMPORARY APPLICATION

Just as my fingerprints are unique to me, so I am unique in the body of Christ. God has gifted me to function in a place prepared especially for me. And I don't have to wait. I can start now!

D. VERSES TO THINK ON THIS WEEK

1 Cor. 12:14–18; 2 Cor. 3:18

E. THOUGHT TO CARRY HOME

I am an important part in the body of Christ. If I don't understand how indispensable I am to the church, I'll lack commitment, and its ministry in the lives of others will be weakened.

F. CREATIVE EXPRESSION

Draw a simple sketch of a church in the space below. Make it look like a picture puzzle by drawing in appropriate lines. Beside it write, "How do I fit into the body?"

Write a prayer asking God to help you find your unique place in His body, your own local church._____

_____

_____

_____

G. SELF-EVALUATION

1. Give a one- or two-word description of yourself in each category.
   a. My personality_____
      1) My greatest strength_____
      2) My greatest weakness_____
   b. My best talent_____
   c. My environment_____
   d. My heritage_____
   e. My greatest interest_____
   f. What I think might be my spiritual gift_____
2. Tell how this lesson has made a difference in the way you see yourself and your church._____

_____

_____

LESSON 34

REACHING OUT TO A LOST WORLD

A. INTRODUCTION

Contrast the destination of those without Christ (Rev. 21:8; 2 Thess. 1:8–10) with those who have been redeemed by Christ's blood (Rev. 21:1–4):

hell

heaven

B. THINKING IT THROUGH

1. What is the gospel message our lost world needs to hear? (1 Cor. 15:3–5)

   a. Write out the plan of salvation by paraphrasing Rom. 3:23; 5:8; 6:23; John 3:16; Rom. 10:13.

   b. Salvation is a gift of God. How does Jesus describe it to the woman at the well? (John 4:10, 13–14)

      To the crowd at the temple? (John 7:37)

      1) The unlimited power of the gospel message to change lives staggers our imaginations. Why do you think Jesus compares it to living water?

2. What specific action verbs do you find in the Great Commission? (Matt. 28:19–20)

   What does this suggest to you?

3. Jesus' command specifies the geographical plan the early church was to follow in reaching their world with the message of the gospel (Acts 1:8). Locate Jerusalem, Judea, and Samaria on a map. What do you think the phrase, *ends of the earth* means?

4. Giving the invitation to those outside the body of Christ means living a life of love. How do we do it? (Rom. 5:5)

5. Jesus modeled this kind of love in John 13:1–8. Write a brief description of His love as you view it from these verses.

6. Write a description of love, paraphrasing Paul's in 1 Cor. 13:4–7?

7. The results of this kind of love are evangelistic (John 13:35). This love sends us into the world with a message and good deeds. Write out Rom. 10:14, 15 and underline the word *sent*.

_____

_____

a. The principle of being a sent one was modeled by Jesus when He_____
   (John 1:14).

b. It's revealed in Jesus' prayer when He prayed, "_____"
   (John 17:18).

c. He commanded it in these words when He commissioned the seventy-two. "_____!
   _____ "(Luke 10:3).

d. To be sent means we go where the hearers are. But building credibility with these hearers take time. How
   did Jesus do it?
   1) Luke 19:5_____
   2) Matt. 9:9, 10_____
   3) John 4:7_____
   4) Matt. 5:2_____

e. Jesus shared himself naturally with those to whom His Father sent Him. Write down two situations in which
   it would be natural for you to verbally share the gospel with a friend.
   1) _____

   _____

   _____

   2) _____

   _____

   _____

8. Look up the following verses and underline the word *come* in Jesus' invitation (Matt. 11:28) and in Jesus'
   promise (John 6:35).

   Jesus said come when He invited the woman at the well to drink. He wanted His disciples to say come to
   everyone He sent them to, to broadcast far and wide that the living water is available to all who would drink.

   The woman asked Jesus, and He gave her that living water. Then her only thirst was to go back to her
   village and say, "_____
   _____." (John 4:29)

9. Write down the last invitation of the Spirit and the church. (Rev. 22:17)_____

   _____

   _____

IT IS YOUR INVITATION, TOO.

C. CONTEMPORARY APPLICATION

Advertisers urge us to take advantage of their offers of free merchandise "today" because their offer expires by
a certain date.

The invitation to "come," to drink deeply, still stands. But someday the offer will be withdrawn. If something
was available for free right now, but later was unavailable, wouldn't you act now? Wouldn't you want your friends
to share the same gift too?

D. VERSES TO THINK ON UNTIL HE COMES

Revelation 22:12–17

E. THOUGHT TO CARRY HOME

If you own a Bible, you have been entrusted with a never-ending supply of living water. Drink deep, then give
it to others.

F. CREATIVE EXPRESSION

As a reminder of your responsibility to freely share the water of life, design an invitation. Invite someone to come
and drink from the water of life.

G. SELF-EVALUATION

1. Do I believe that this message is the most important one in the world? Why or why not?
2. How is my life different from one who doesn't accept Christ's offer to come?
3. What person heading for the fiery lake will I begin to make my friend this week?
4. How will I share the message of the gospel with them?